Number Dete

Patterns, Functions, and Structures

Catherine Twomey Fosnot

New Perspectives on Learning, LLC
1194 Ocean Avenue
New London, CT 06320

ISBN-13: 978-1-7335321-0-5

Table of Contents

Unit Overview

The focus of this unit is the extension of operations to algebraic reasoning by gaining familiarity with common factors and multiples, generating and analyzing patterns and sequences, and exploring the importance of primes as they relate to composites. The unit also supports a unification of the strand of number and operation with the strand of geometry. Students learn about the mystery of triangular numbers and the possibility of a hidden double agent. They build a sequence of the triangular numbers and examine patterns in it. They transform quantities into geometric shapes, explore sequences of squares and cubes of primes, and eventually are introduced to the Fibonacci sequence and the related spiral, where the mystery and wonders of number are connected to the beauty and regularity of nature around them.

The unit is designed to align with the CCSS Standards of Practice and the following core objectives:

Operations & Algebraic Thinking 4.OA

Use operations with whole numbers to solve problems.

CCSS.MATH.CONTENT.4.OA.A.1

Interpret a multiplication equation as a comparison, e.g., interpret 35 = 5 × 7 as a statement that 35 is 5 times as many as 7 and 7 times as many as 5. Represent verbal statements of multiplicative comparisons as multiplication equations.

CCSS.MATH.CONTENT.4.OA.A.2

Multiply or divide to solve word problems involving multiplicative comparison, e.g., by using drawings and equations with a symbol for the unknown number to represent the problem, distinguishing multiplicative comparison from additive comparison.

Gain familiarity with factors and multiples.

CCSS.MATH.CONTENT.4.OA.B.4

Find all factor pairs for a whole number in the range 1-100. Recognize that a whole number is a multiple of each of its factors. Determine whether a given whole number in the range 1-100 is a multiple of a given one-digit number. Determine whether a given whole number in the range 1-100 is prime or composite.

Generate and analyze patterns.

CCSS.MATH.CONTENT.4.OA.C.5

Generate a number or shape pattern that follows a given rule. Identify apparent features of the pattern that were not explicit in the rule itself. *For example, given the rule "Add 3" and the starting number 1, generate terms in the resulting sequence and observe that the terms appear to alternate between odd and even numbers. Explain informally why the numbers will continue to alternate in this way.*

The Mathematical Landscape

Number Detectives is designed to support the further development of operations and algebraic thinking by involving students in structuring the number system multiplicatively, investigating common factors and multiples, sorting numbers into primes and composites, analyzing patterns and sequences, and even representing some quantities and sequences as geometric forms.

This unit also builds a strong foundational understanding of the connection between factors and divisors, and several minilessons are used to support division strategies for computational fluency. For example, students note patterns in the multiples, which fosters the raising of conjectures about divisibility rules. They note how doubling a divisor halves the quotient; and halving the divisor doubles the quotient. They explore how common factors and multiples are formed when numbers are multiplied. For example, they note how 6x5 can be thought of as 2x3x5, and thus the product of 30 has factors produced from 2x3, 2x5, and 3x5, as well as 1, 2, 3, 5, and 30; they note how when 2 factors are multiplied the product is a multiple of both factors and when the multiple is divided by one of the factors, the quotient is the other, because of the relationship between multiplication and division.

Our number system is a beautiful invention. It is a multiplicative system based on the powers of ten; but, it is also based on prime factorization. Fully understanding prime factorization is not the goal of this unit—that goal will be on the horizon for students in later years. However, as students explore primes and composites many opportunities present themselves whereby some big ideas and strategies that underlie prime factorization begin to emerge. Students experience how primes can be squared and cubed and how doing so affects the number of factors the products of each have. As they investigate common factors and multiples, they begin to understand why they occur. Exploring factors and multiples also helps to support fluency with the basic facts.

One of the important standards of mathematical practice is the search for structure and regularity. This search gets to the heart of what mathematicians do and to the resulting feelings of aesthetic beauty when structures are built and uncovered. As students learn to treat the solving of interesting cases with deductive reasoning, collection of evidence, and the development of proof as detectives, they come to understand the joys and similarities of the practices to mathematics. As students transform numbers into exquisite geometric forms found in nature, they come to marvel at how mathematics is a powerful lens to understand the world they live in.

As you work through this unit there are several big ideas, strategies, and models on the journey to encourage and celebrate. Figure 1 lists the landmarks of development that you will likely see your students constructing and using as you progress through the unit. A description of each follows.

The fuller landscape of multiplication and division is provided on page 11 so that you can situate the development you will likely see with this unit, on the fuller journey your students will travel as they develop an understanding of multiplication and division through the years.

The Landscape of Learning

BIG IDEAS
❖ Place value patterns occur when multiplying by ten
❖ The commutative property of multiplication
❖ The associative property of multiplication
❖ The distributive property of multiplication
❖ The relationship between multiplication and division
❖ Place value patterns occur when dividing by ten
❖ Proportional reasoning
❖ The generalized use of the distributive property of multiplication in solving division problems
❖ The dimensions of length and width can be used to produce a square unit measurement of area
❖ The dimensions of length, width, and height can be used to produce a cubic unit measurement of volume
STRATEGIES
❖ Skipcounting
❖ Using ten-times
❖ Using partial products
❖ Using partial quotients
❖ Use of automatized facts
❖ Factoring and grouping flexibly
MODELS
❖ Additive structuring
❖ Multiplicative structuring
❖ Open number line
❖ Open arrays
❖ Ratio tables

Figure 1

BIG IDEAS

As children explore the investigations within this unit, several big ideas will likely arise. These include:

❖ *Place value patterns occur when multiplying by ten*

An interesting thing happens when we multiply by the base—the factor bumps over to the appropriate column. For example, consider 10x4 = 4+4+4+4+4+4+4+4+4+4. The result of 40 can seem like magic to children, who often say that they added a zero to the 4. When challenged, they will agree they did not really "add" a zero; they just placed it on the right of the number they were multiplying. Noticing this pattern is important, but sadly most students have little understanding of why this pattern occurs. The reason this action works is that we can think of the ten groups of four as four groups of ten (the commutative property)—so the value (in this case 4) moves to the left into the ten's column. Likewise, 100x8 = 8x100, so the 8 moves left to the hundred's column. It is important to support students in exploring why this pattern happens—to help them construct how place value and the commutative property are involved.

❖ *The commutative property of multiplication*

Multiplication is commutative: a x b = b x a. Picture four towers, each made with nineteen connecting cubes. Now imagine them right next to each other so they make a 4x19 rectangular array. If we turn this array ninety degrees, we have a 19x4 array—nineteen towers with four cubes in each. Using arrays like this is exactly what students do to convince each other of the commutative property. Students may have constructed this property earlier, but they may not have related it to the place value patterns that occur when multiplying by ten. They also may not realize how it is connected to common multiples: 6x3 = 3x6 so 18 is a common multiple of 6 and 3.

❖ *The associative property of multiplication*

As your students work with the investigations in this unit, they will begin to understand that a number can be formed by several factors. For example, 2x2x2x2 can be thought of as (2x2)x(2x2) = 4x4, a square number. It can also be thought of as 2x(2x2x2) = 2x8, two cubes. All the factors are there; only the parentheses have moved. In fact, the parentheses can be moved to a variety of places because the associative property holds for multiplication. This property also explains how factors of a number can be found. For example, 30 can be thought of as 1x2x3x5. When you associate the factors in all the possible arrangements, you get all the factors—1, 2, 3, 5, 6, 10, 15, and 30.

❖ *The distributive property of multiplication*

Multiplication can be distributed over both addition and subtraction. For example, 19 x 4 can be thought of as 10x4 + 9x4, and as 20x4 – 1x4. In this unit, as students explore divisibility rules, the property comes in very handy. Consider division by 4. Every hundred, no matter how many hundreds a number has, can be thought of as 4x25. Thus, if the remaining portion of the number is divisible by 4, the whole number is. For example, 344 can be thought of as 100/4 + 100/4 + 100/4 + 44/4, or as 4x75 + 4x11. Generalized to even larger numbers, everything to the left of the ten's place is a hundred: 1,224 = 12 hundreds + 24.

❖ *The relationship between multiplication and division*

Division is defined as the inverse of multiplication. Students extend their understanding of these operations when they consider the relationship between them and the relationship between factors and divisors. An important multiplicative structure of part-whole relations is at play here. The factors when multiplied produce the product; the product when divided by a factor produces the other factor. Representing the operations using arrays and examining the relationship between factors and divisors helps students understand how multiplication and division are related.

❖ *Place value patterns occur when dividing by ten*

When dividing by ten, one can just shift the value to the right. As students explore divisibility rules in this unit, they quickly come to see that multiples of ten all end in 0, and when a multiple of 10 is shifted to the right, the quotient is left. For example, consider 320/10. The dividend of 320 moves to the right and becomes 32.0.

❖ *Proportional reasoning*

In this unit as students explore division strategies, they note that when the divisor doubles the quotient halves. Reciprocally, when the divisor halves the quotient doubles. These are examples of proportional reasoning.

❖ *The generalized use of the distributive property of multiplication in solving division problems*

The big idea underlying why the standard long division algorithm works is the distributive property of multiplication. Partial products can be made. For example, when dividing 328 by 8, students can use 8x40 and 8x1.

❖ *The dimensions of length and width can be used to produce a square unit measurement of area*

Counting objects in rows and columns is easier for students than understanding that the area covered can be measured in square units determined by linear units used to measure length and width. Research by Battista (1998), suggests that an array model is often difficult for learners to understand because it requires a substantial cognitive reorganization requiring the consideration of rows and columns simultaneously. For this reason, in this unit rectangular arrays are used as a representational model and they are described as an arrangement of rows and columns.

❖ *The dimensions of length, width, and height can be used to produce a cubic unit measurement of volume*

The measurement of three-dimensional space is even more difficult. Determining the shape of the cubic unit that is created can be quite elusive. As students explore and mathematize the situations in this unit, they will grapple with how 2x2x2 or 3x3x3 become cubes. It will help to model the shape with inch cubes. In this unit, students are only asked to consider how a number can be transformed into a cube, and they build a sequence of cube numbers. The formula for volume measurement is not an intended purpose of this unit. The CFLM unit *The Box Factory* (a grade 5 unit) is designed with that purpose in mind. In that unit, students build boxes, consider surface area, and the more generalized formula for volume measurement and surface area are constructed.

STRATEGIES

As you work with the activities in this unit, you will notice that students will use many strategies to solve the problems that are posed to them. Here are some strategies to notice:

❖ *Skipcounting*

To figure out the common multiples along a pathway to the crime scene (investigation #1 in this unit), many students will start by skipcounting by twos and skipcounting by fours, then skipcounting by threes. They may not join or coordinate the common landing points at first, as they are focused solely on skipcounting along the path. The open number line model and the context of common meeting places used in the unit will help, and over time, students will build a more useful set of strategies relying on regrouping factors and using equivalent expressions to find common multiples.

❖ *Using ten-times*

As students explore divisibility rules, the use of ten times will help them construct a divisibility rule for 9. Using the distributive property for multiplication over subtraction, 27 is seen as 10x3-3, and 18 is 10x2-2, etc. Therefore, 27 must be divisible by 9 because in each of the 2 tens there will be 1 unit remaining when the tens are divided by 9, and if the units remaining when added to the other units make another group of 9, the number is divisible by 9. For example, the sum of the digits (2+7) equals 9, so 27 must be divisible by 9 as it is a multiple of 9.

❖ *Using partial products and partial quotients*

Students will likely already be using partial products when multiplying before you begin this unit. This strategy however needs to be generalized to develop some of the divisibility rules they will explore in this unit. For example, since there are 25 fours in every hundred, when determining if a number is divisible by 4 one only has to look at the remaining 2 digits (in the ten's and unit's columns). If that amount is divisible by 4 the whole number is. For example, 324 is divisible by 4 because the hundreds are and 24 is:
300/4 + 24/4 = 75 + 6.

❖ *Use of automatized facts*

Many students may have the basic facts automatic already; but many may not. Notice as you progress through the unit, who does and who doesn't. You will likely see progress towards automaticity as students work with factors every day because they will be building a network of related facts.

❖ *Factoring and grouping flexibly*

By the end of the unit you will likely see students much more able to find factors and associate them flexibly in different ways to find other factors and to produce common multiples.

❖ *Additive structuring*

The first modeling of the number system is additive. Children are challenged just by decomposing amounts. They do not see 132 as 13 tens + 2. They see it as 100 + 30 + 2. They decompose using expanded notation. Likewise, when they analyze sequences, they start with addition first, also. They analyze sequences additively, looking at the differences between the terms in a sequence. When looking for patterns on a ratio table they analyze the differences moving down the righthand column.

❖ *Multiplicative structuring*

It is a huge leap in development when students begin to consider multiplicative functions. As students begin to relate input to output and see that each input has been multiplied by the same factor to produce the output, they are building a sense of ratio. They move across a ratio table as well as down it. When they analyze a sequence, they consider the operations of multiplication and division.

❖ *Model of a situation*

Initially models emerge as a representation *of* a situation; later they are used by teachers to represent children's strategies. Ultimately, they are appropriated by children as powerful tools *for* thinking (Gravemeijer 1999). In this unit students begin by exploring common factors and multiples as places where several footprints of suspects are found. **The open number line model** emerges as a model of the pathway. It is used to support students to look for common meeting places of numbers along a pathway. Students are also provided with a database in the form of a **ratio table**. Later, as students begin to explore primes and composites, **the open array** is used to model the transformations of numbers into a variety of shapes.

❖ *Model of Student Strategies*

In this unit, the open array is also used to represent student strategies during minilessons. Representations like these provide a chance for students to see and understand their peers' strategies and how one arrangement of factors produces the same area as another set.

❖ *Models as Tools for Thinking*

Eventually students become able to use the models as tools for thinking about geometric relationships; they are able to imagine the geometric shapes as both quantities and shapes. But most importantly, as your students become able to represent geometric relations, the models will in fact become not just representations of the shapes they make, but abstract objects and tools *for* thinking.

References and Resources

Gravemeijer, Koeno (1999). How emergent models may foster the constitution of formal mathematics. *Mathematical Thinking and Learning 1* (2): 155–77.

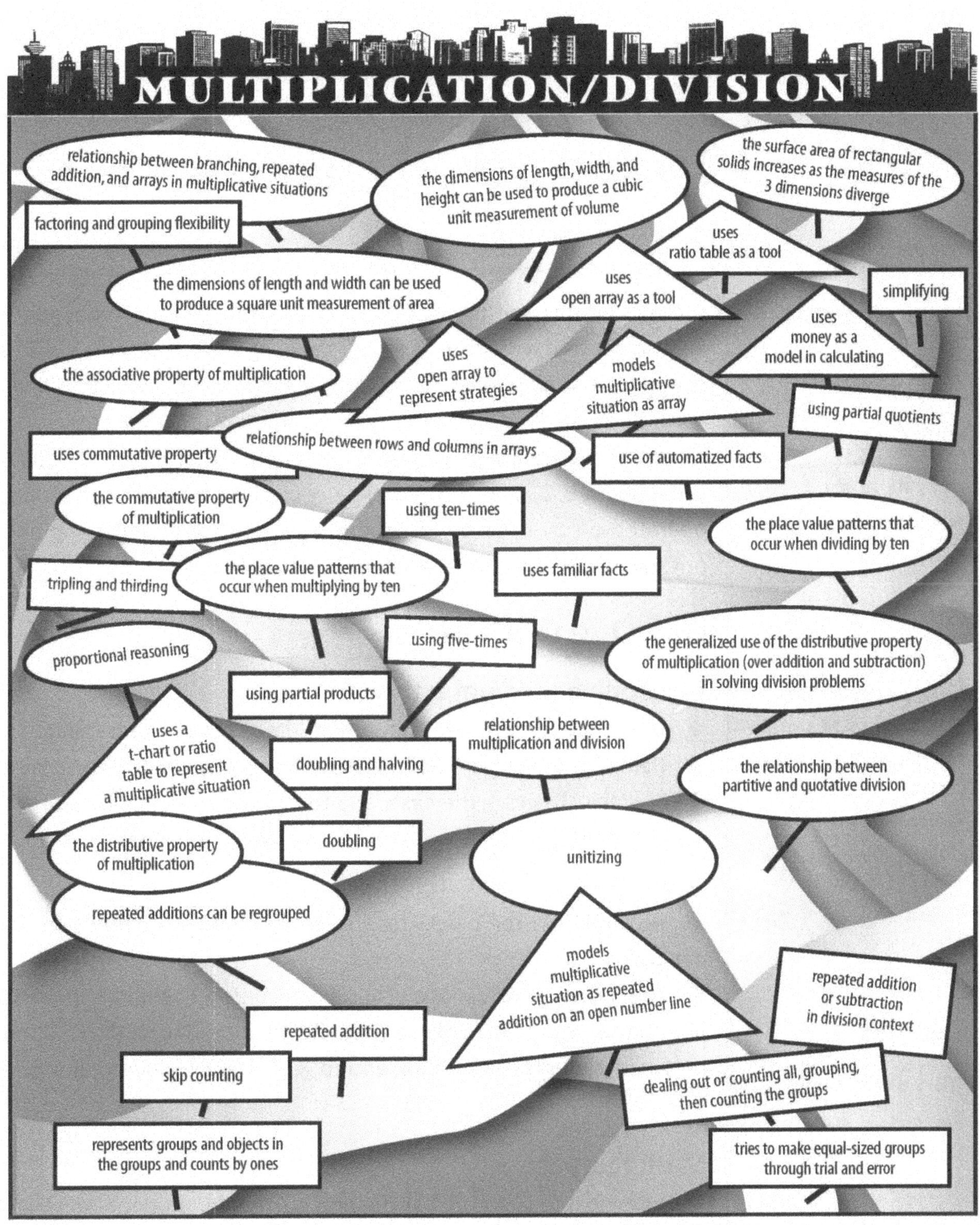

The landscape of learning: multiplication and division on the horizon showing landmark strategies (rectangles), big ideas (ovals), and models (triangles).

Figure 2

DAY ONE

OPERATING WITH 2, 3, AND 4

Materials Needed

Detective Pairs (Appendix A)

Mystery #1 and Some Clues (Appendix B)

Base-10 blocks, one set per pair of students consisting of:
- ***1 Block of 1,000***
- ***10 Flats of 100***
- ***10 Rods of 10***
- ***10 unit cubes***

Scissors (one per pair of students)

graph paper

Math Journals

Markers and Pencils

The unit begins with the formation of pairs of detectives who will work throughout this unit to crack some number mysteries. Today, detectives are presented with the case of #322, the spot where a crime was committed. Who was there, #2, #3, or #4? Is there a way to tell whether a whole number is divisible by 2, or if the number has already been multiplied by 2? Could 322 be in a sequence that begins 0, 2, 4, 6, 8...? What about 0, 3, 6, 9...? Are there any patterns when a number has been operated on by 4, or by 3? Students work in pairs collecting evidence, putting forth conjectures, and offering proofs.

Day One Outline

Developing the Context

❖ Introduce the context of number detectives and form pairs.

❖ Pass out Appendix A with pictures and Appendix B with some clues.

❖ Ask pairs to crack the case, and to provide evidence they are right.

Supporting the Investigation

❖ Provide base-ten blocks for students to model the problem as needed.

❖ As students work, move around and confer. Encourage them to note patterns in the multiples (particularly considering the relationship between multiples of 2 and 4, and to generate divisibility rules for both).

Math Journals

❖ Provide a few minutes at the end of class for students to reflect and work to articulate their learning from the day.

Developing the Context

In this unit students will take on the roles of detectives. Start by explaining what detectives do:

A detective is an investigator. Detectives most often work in pairs. They collect information to solve a case by examining clues, collecting physical evidence, and searching records in databases. Sometimes they make their own database. This leads them to the examining of patterns, the uncovering of clues, and the putting forth of conjectures, which they then work to prove. As they work on a case, they take notes.

Explain that you have assigned pairs of detectives, and then pass out a copy of Appendix A to each pair.

Explain that each pair will work on the case. Some clues are given, but they will need to find more as they work and keep track of them in their math journals. As they work, they should look for patterns in the numbers. Finding patterns will help them crack cases faster. At the end, when they think they have solved the case, they should work on a way to prove and justify the solution.

Pass out Appendix B, explaining that a crime has been reported at location #322. There are three suspects under surveillance: the number 2, the number 3, and the number 4. There are also several clues given, and they should work to uncover more. Could all 3 suspects have been at location #322? The footprints along the pathway are nice clues of where the numbers have been and will help students solve the case. The databases might be helpful, too. Two databases are provided, and they can build others if they wish.

If students feel stuck, suggest that modeling the situation can sometimes be helpful. Drawing paper and base ten blocks are provided if they want to do so.

Teacher Note:

It's not necessary, but it is a lot of fun to start with pictures of each student pasted onto Appendix A with their names written next to the picture. The easiest way to do this is to take a picture of each student with your cell the day before you begin the unit. Close ups of just the faces are best. E-mail the pics to yourself and then insert them into a doc file as a pic. Using the "picture tools" function you can frame the pics. An example is shown below. Print the pics out and cut and paste them onto Appendix A.

Supporting the Investigation

Let students get settled and ensure everyone understands the goal of the investigation. Then listen in on some conversations. Here are some strategies and big ideas you are likely to see emerging:

- Skipcounting by 2s, 3s, and 4s. This strategy can become very tedious, although it can be helpful to students if they start noticing patterns—for example, they might start noticing common multiples of 2, 3, and 4, or patterns in the sequences themselves. In the long run, generating multiples will help students become familiar with multiples and this will help with the eventual automatization of the multiplication facts. For this reason, let students skipcount a bit if that is the strategy with which they begin. As you confer, encourage them to look for patterns though, reminding them that noting patterns and looking for clues is what detectives do. You might ask students if they see any relationships between the numbers. For example, do they notice that every other multiple of 2 is a multiple of 4? Students often say, "When skipcounting by 4s, you skip every other number that you said when you skip counted by 2s!"

- Some students may have a strong sense of even and odd numbers and may start by using it, saying, "All even numbers end in 0, 2, 4, 6, or 8. Since 322 ends in 2, #2 must be the culprit." Ask them what happens with 4s and 3s. Do they ever land on numbers that end in 2? And if so, why are they ruling out 3s and 4s? Maybe all 3 suspects were involved? Encourage them to dig for more clues, such as common meeting points where several footprints might be found. Suggest they use the base ten sticks (or an open number line) to model the pathway and mark the common points where more than one suspect has been. Can they predict more common meeting points? Ask them if they found any interesting clues in the databases and if so encourage them to make a database for 4.
- Some students may model the pathway to the crime scene using a double number line. This is a powerful model to use to explore common multiples as the common landing points can be shown. Note how students use this model though; many students often show the jumps but not the common landing points (see Figure 3) because they are so focused on the skipcounting. As you confer, question them about where they are placing the numbers and if there any common landing points—places where footprints would meet (as shown at the beginning of the pathway on Appendix B). Then, challenge them to figure out why those common points happened and encourage them to predict more.

Figure 3: Double number line with skipcounting, but common meeting points not shown

- Other students may use facts they know and work from there, by doubling or using partial products. For example, they may say, "4 will land on 40, because that is ten times. So, it will land on 80 and then 160, and then 320. It can't land on 322 if it lands on 320 because it is only 2 more, not 4." Others might say, "4 will land on 100 because there are 4 quarters in a dollar, so 200 and 300 are stopping places, too. This is a nice insight. Push for a generalization. Ask if 4 goes into every hundred evenly, no matter how many hundreds there are. Base ten blocks are provided as they serve as nice tools for investigating this. Every pallet has 4 x 25 in it so it doesn't matter how many pallets there are. All one needs to do is look at the remainder—the digits in the first two columns. In the case of

322, there are 22 left and that amount is not divisible by 4 evenly, so #4 could not have landed on the crime scene location, spot #322, and is not the culprit. Could #3 be the culprit? 300 also divides evenly by 3, and it does not divide evenly into 22, so #3 is not the culprit either.

Math Note:

Some powerful mathematics can be uncovered and justified in this investigation. All numbers that are multiples of 2, end in 0, 2, 4, 6, or 8 and all multiples of 2 are even. But the same can be said about the multiples of 4. This is because 4 = 2 x 2. Every other multiple of 2 is a multiple of 4. Every other multiple of 3 is an even number, too, because it is also a multiple of 2. Thus, many multiples of 3 also end in 0, 2, 4, 6, 8. Let's think about a divisibility rule for 4. If 100 can be divided by 4 evenly, then any number of hundreds is also divisible by 4. This means if the last 2 digits are divisible by 4, the whole number is. 320 and 324 are both divisible by 4, because 300/4 works and 20/4 works (also 24/4). But 322 is not divisible by 4, because 22 is not. The divisibility rule for 3 is a little more challenging. In every hundred there is always 1 left over because 99/3 works. There is also 1 left over in the 10 because 9/3 works. Thus, if one adds the remainders (which really are the digits—3 in the hundreds, 2 in the tens, and 2 in the units), if the sum is also divisible by 3, the whole number is. This rule is much more challenging for fourth graders to construct and thus it is not the focus of today's work. It is helpful however helpful for you to know the rule because your children may surprise you!

Inside One Classroom: Conferring with Students at Work

Camille (the teacher): I'm so interested in the strategy that you are working on. May I sit and confer with you? It looks like you are skipcounting. Am I right?

Sydney: Yes.

James: We are skipcounting by 2s, and then we are going to do 4s and 3s. Then we'll know which numbers land on 322.

Camille: Wow! So, if the number doesn't land on 322 you know it can't be that number? Great strategy! It's going to take a long time, though, right? Skipcounting to 322 is not easy! Have you considered a way to model the pathway to see if there are any patterns?

James: What do you mean?

Camille: Well, sometimes it helps as a number detective to model the situation. For example, you might draw the pathway like an open number line. You could do skipcounting by 2s on the bottom and skipcounting by 4s on the top, like on the sheet. I don't know if it would be

Author's notes

As Camille confers, notice how she starts the conferral by listening and getting clarification.

Note how Camille suggests modeling, and even a specific one. Mentors often make suggestions, but it is always up to the mathematicians to determine if

helpful or not, but it might show some common places they land that might save a lot of work. **Sydney:** Well, I know they both land on 100. Because there are 4 quarters in 100. And 50 plus 50 is 100. **Camille:** Wow! What a great way to think about it! You could start your number line with 100 then instead of having to do all the skipcounting because you already know both 2 and 4 land on 100! So, if they land on 100, will they also land on 200? What do you think, James? **James:** Maybe. *(He starts skipcounting on from 100).* **Camille:** What do you think, Sydney? Will James get 2 and 4 to both land on 200? **Sydney:** *(Pondering at first).* I think they have to land there, James. It's just another 100. They will land on 300, too. **Camille:** What do you think, James? Is she right? **James:** *(Pondering but then grinning).* Oh yeah! Wow! That did save time! And now we just have 22 more to go. **Sydney:** Oh... oh! I think I get it! The culprit has to be 2 because 2 goes into 22. But 4 doesn't. 4 will land on 20 and 24, but not on 22. Remember, James? When we were skipcounting by 2s and 4s? That is what happened. **Camille:** Wow! Hmmm.... Are you saying that it doesn't matter how many hundreds you have because 4 will always go into the hundreds? Do you only have to look at the part that is left and if 4 goes into that part, too, you'll land there? At the bottom of this sheet it says, "Is there a way to tell ahead if a number is divisible by 4?" I think you might have a way of answering that question already!! But I'll leave you to think about that because I want to get to some other pairs of students, too, ok? But let me know what you find out. Wow! Very exciting! You are great number detectives!!	*they want to pursue that direction. Ownership is critical.* *Camille asks a powerful question here. Encouraging James to consider what Sydney has said is also important and will engender even deeper thinking and reflection. And, it ensures the conferral includes both students in the thinking.* *Camille celebrates what the students have done. Then she leaves them to think. They have hit on something big—a divisibility rule for 4! But they will need time to ponder it before they will be able to explain it to others and justify it. By going off she provides them with that time.*

Math Journals

During the last five minutes of class, ask students to write in their math journals about the big "a-ha" moments or discoveries they had today. Taking the time to reflect will help them hold on to their ideas, expose areas of confusion, and set the stage for tomorrow's work. Reading these entries will help you, the teacher, see where each student is on the landscape of learning. This information will help you plan conferrals for tomorrow and understand what happened for the students that you didn't get to confer with today. Towards that aim, ask students,

> *"Before we end for today, write about your latest thinking so that you can hold on to it. What are the big ideas you are working on? I will read what you wrote and write back to you."*

Before the next class, read the entries and respond to each mathematician at least briefly with a question or prompt to strengthen or challenge thinking. Use the strategies and big ideas on the landscape of learning described in the Overview section of the unit as a guide.

Reflections on the Day

Today, students worked as "number detectives" on their first case. They explored 3 sequences, looked for common multiples, and investigated why they were occurring. They looked for patterns in the sequences and explored the functions and data in ratio tables. They have likely noticed several patterns. Some may even have constructed divisibility rules for 2 and 4. Others may not have yet; they may have spent a lot of time skipcounting. That is ok at this point in the unit. Skipcounting itself can be challenging and the more they do it, the easier it will become. Familiarity with skipcounting and the multiples that result will also help students with their developing number sense, and with the eventual automatization of the basic facts. So, don't be too concerned if no one has ventured forth with a divisibility rule yet. For now, just keep interest going in cracking the case—keep it a mystery. Note the many ideas and strategies you witnessed emerging today and think about the gallery walk and math congress that you will hold tomorrow. Which strategies and ideas would be powerful to discuss? Which posters will you use, and in which order, to ensure a rich, growth-producing conversation for everyone?

DAY TWO

THE CASE IS CRACKED

Materials Needed

Students' work from Day One

Extra copies of Appendix B to use as needed

Lined sticky notes, several per student

Math Journals

Poster paper

Markers and Pencils

Today begins with students reading their math journals and noting the comments and entries you made as you reflected on what they wrote at the end of math workshop yesterday. Then students meet in peer review groups to share and discuss the clues/patterns they have found thus far, culminating with the making of a group poster for a subsequent gallery walk and congress. The focus of the congress is on the solution to the case and the justifications given by the detectives, with emphasis placed on the patterns students have noticed, the ways they modeled the case, and a comparison and examination of the databases.

Day Two Outline

Math Journals

❖ Provide quiet time with math journals for students to read the comments they have received and to revisit their own reflections from the previous day.

❖ Have students finish their work and make a poster. Journals will be used again after the math congress.

Facilitating the Gallery Walk

❖ Confer with children as they put finishing touches to their posters, asking them to consider the most important things they want to tell their audience about the case. Emphasize the importance of justifying their solutions.

❖ Conduct a gallery walk to allow students time to reflect and comment on each other's posters.

Facilitating the Math Congress

❖ Convene students at the meeting area to discuss a few important noticings, such as patterns and regularities they noticed when they examined the databases and common meeting points.

Math Journals

Provide students about 5-10 minutes to read over your responses to their journal entries from Day One. This time will also prepare them to return to their work if they are not yet finished. If most have finished, pass out chart paper and invite them to work on posters for a gallery and congress. Remind them that, as good detectives, they will need to prove their solution to the case as well.

Facilitating the Gallery Walk

As students work on posters, move around and confer, asking them to consider the most important things they want to tell their audience about the structure and regularities they noticed in the database and about where footprints meet (common multiples). Remind them that it is not necessary to write about everything they did, but instead to concentrate on convincing their audience about the important things they discovered and want to defend. As good detectives, they need to prove and justify their solution to the case. They need to present evidence.

The main purpose of a gallery walk is the development of the reading and writing of viable arguments, but it is also to provide time for reflection, refinement, and consolidation of the thinking learners generated as they worked on the investigation. When students are postering, the ideas they write about often go *beyond describing what they did*, to *the writing about their breakthroughs, new ideas, and insights*. Encourage students in this work (rather than emphasizing or requesting that they write about their steps from start to finish). Doing this will support their development toward competent writing of convincing mathematical arguments. As you move around conferring and helping your students get ready for the gallery walk, look for moments where you can facilitate and support the development of big ideas and justifications for their generalization.

The students' role in the gallery walk is an important one. Their thoughtful consideration of another's work in this community of mathematicians can help them to deepen their own thinking, to question the validity of their peers' mathematical arguments, and to develop new strategies. Spend some time helping students develop language for responding to the posters and establish guidelines for gallery walks. Sentence frames such as "I agree with ___ because ___" and "I have a question about ___" are more helpful than brief notes, like "nice job," or "I agree." Emphasize a quiet atmosphere so that all reviewers can read and think before commenting. This time should be taken seriously. Ask students to start at different places and choose three or four posters to focus on, recording their comments on lined sticky notes arranged on a clipboard. Encourage them to spread out so that all posters will have at least a few comments. After about ten minutes, ask them to finish up their final notes and return to their own posters to read the feedback they were given. Provide time to revise work if needed, based on the feedback received.

During the gallery walk it's important that you make comments on posters as well, so that students see you as a member of the community who is really interested in their thinking. Look for moments and places where you can show your students that you are seriously trying to understand their thinking and remember, you are their mentor. Appreciate their good thinking, comment on interesting approaches, and suggest where more detail could be helpful to support understanding. Raise questions that might push for generalization or further insights. As you move around, look for big ideas and strategies from the landscape. This will help you to plan which pieces of work you will select for the congress, if you haven't done that already.

Facilitating the Math Congress

Review the posters and choose a few that you can use for a discussion that will deepen understanding and support growth along the landscape of learning described in the Overview. There is not necessarily one best plan for a congress. There are many different plans that might all be supportive of development. You'll want to focus the congress on the structure and regularities students noticed, such as how the meeting points of #2 and #4 can be found at every other multiple of 2 and/or why the common multiples of 2, 3, and 4 are all multiples of 12. The question about divisibility rules for 2 and 4 should also be discussed in the congress if it is emerging. A rule for 2 will likely be easy for most students, as by fourth grade many students will have explored even numbers and will know they end in 0, 2, 4, 6, 8. Challenge students to dig deeper though and to explain why. Do they realize that even numbers also divide into 2 equal groups—that *N2 = 2N*? When they discuss divisibility rules for 4, challenge them for a justification. The noticing of the pattern of every other multiple of 2 is important as you examine common multiples, but it isn't sufficient as a divisibility rule. You'll want to focus discussion on the divisibility of all hundreds by 4, and thus all that matters for a determination is a consideration of the last 2 digits. This requires looking at the division as partial quotients: 300/4 + 22/4. The underlying big idea to justify partial quotients is the distributive property of multiplication. If 22/4 did not have a remainder, 322 would have been divisible by 4 evenly, but it does. 320 and 324 are both multiples of 4 because 20 and 24 are divisible by 4. A window into one classroom follows as an example. The work under discussion can be seen in Figure 4, below.

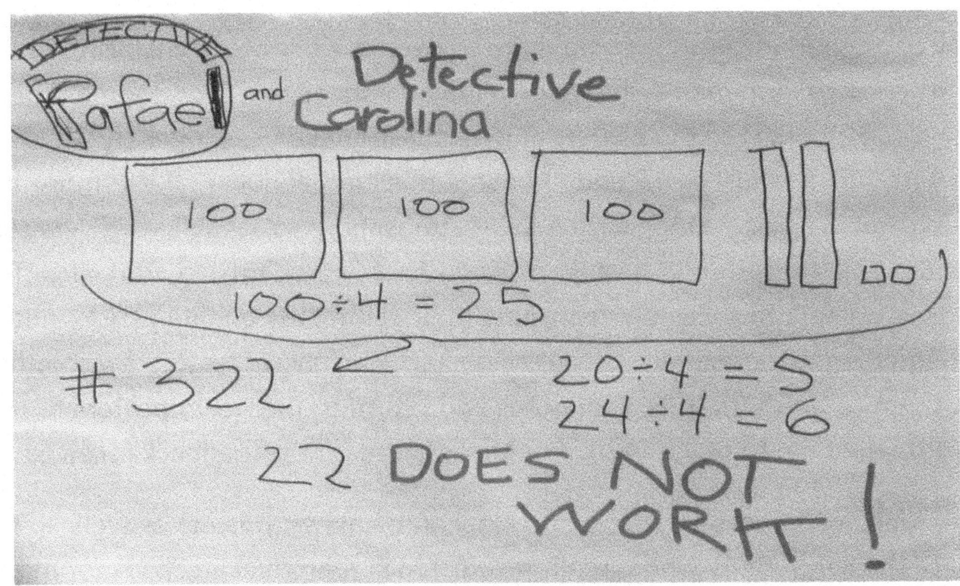

Figure 4: Student work being discussed in the dialogue box on page 21

Inside One Classroom: A Portion of the Math Congress

Camille (the teacher): Ok, we've heard from Noah and Maia who convinced us that the culprit was #2. They produced evidence that #3 and #4 could not have left footprints at the crime scene. So now let's turn the conversation to the big questions at the bottom of the sheet. Is there a way that we could just have known ahead whether 322 was divisible by 2, 3, or 4? Tanika?

Tanika: Numbers that can be divided by 2 end in 0, 2, 4, 6, and 8.

Camille: Why is that? Does anyone know?

Noah: Because those are even numbers. You are skipcounting by twos, so you can never land on odd numbers. Also, dividing by two is like splitting the number in half. Like 30/2 is 15 and 20/2 is 10.

Maia: 15 ends in 5.

Noah: Yeah, but the answer doesn't have to end in 0, 2, 4, 6, or 8. Only the 30 matters. It ends in 0 and so it is even and can be divided by 2.

Camille: Wow! Put your hand up if you understand what Noah means. Let's all turn to a partner and help each other understand what he said. *(After a few minutes of pair talk, Camille resumes whole group discussion.)* Ok, let's come back together and see if we can figure this out. Did anyone have a helpful partner? Tammy?

Tammy: Sydney and I agree. We think it is just like what Noah said. Even numbers are doubles. 15 + 15 = 30, so 30 can be divided by 2.

Camille: So, how does 4 fit into this? How do we know if a number is divisible by 4? Ben?

Ben: We looked at the database. The fours and twos are related. Every other two was in the fours.

Camille: Interesting! Who else noticed that? (several hands go up). Did anyone figure out why? Anthony?

Anthony: I think because 2 x 2 = 4. So, fours are always double of the twos.

Maia: Oh, I get it! That's cool.

Camille: Wow! So many regularities! Patterns and relationships everywhere!! This is what makes math so

Author's notes

Camille chooses to start the congress with a discussion by Noah and Maia on their solution and their evidence. They skip counted by each number and found that #3 and #4 could not have left footprints on 322. A conversation like this will be beneficial for all. But then Camille goes to the heart of the matter. She asks, "Is there a way that we could just have known ahead whether 322 was divisible by 2, 3, or 4? "

Asking if anyone had a helpful partner implicitly sends the message that pair talk needs to be accountable talk.

Camille challenges, "How does 4 fit into this? How do we know if a number is divisible by 4?"

Notice how Camille expresses joy over finding patterns? She even introduces the words regularities

much fun, isn't it? The structures we discover!! So, let's examine fours a little more. Rafael and Carolina, bring your poster up and explain what you did. Rafael and Carolina had an interesting idea about the fours. See what you think. **Carolina:** We used the blocks and so we had 3 pallets, 2 sticks, and 2 units. We knew 100 would be divisible by 4 because we know 4 x 25 = 100. Do you want to tell the next part, Rafael? **Rafael:** Then we realized all the hundreds would be divisible by 4. It doesn't matter how many you have. They are all pallets. You only have to look at what is left. 22 is left. If it had been 20 or 24, #4 could have been there. But 322 is not divisible by 4 because 22 isn't divisible by 4.	*and structure—one of the important standards of mathematical practice.* *Carolina and Rafael have discovered and justified nicely the divisibility rule for 4.*

Math Journals

At the end of the congress, provide everyone with some further reflective writing time. You might ask students to write about an idea they thought was particularly powerful, a new idea they are now thinking about, or the connections they see between the posters shared. What do they understand about common multiples? Or, divisibility rules? Giving students time to articulate their new understandings will also provide you with important information that you can use as formative assessment. Take the journals home again tonight and read over the entries. Comment on them. Dialoguing in journals can be very powerful to keep thinking going and it is a great way to do assessment. Take a pic of the entry as evidence of learning!

Reflections on the Day

Math workshop began today with students looking at the comments they received in their journals, considering the questions and challenges posed, and extending or justifying ideas. They continued deepening their understanding in peer review groups and by refining their own posters and carefully considering the work of their classmates during the gallery walk. The congress helped to solidify and extend everyone's understanding of factors, common multiples, and divisibility rules. Giving children time to review their ideas, to justify their thinking, to extend their thinking to other examples, and to learn from each other's work contributes to the development of these young mathematicians in powerful ways, and the classroom becomes a true mathematics laboratory.

DAY THREE

AGENT #9 HOLDS A MEETING

The day begins with a "count-around" minilesson designed to focus discussion on multiples of 10, and then 9. The minilesson serves also as a foundation for a new mystery involving agents #2, #3, #4, #5, #6, and #10, where students explore common meeting points (common multiples) and crack the secret codes of the agents (more divisibility rules).

Materials Needed

Mystery #2 (Appendix C), one copy per pair of students

Drawing paper and markers

Base-10 blocks, one set per pair of students consisting of:
- ***1 Block of 1,000***
- ***10 Flats of 100***
- ***10 Rods of 10***
- ***10 unit cubes***

Math Journals

Pencils

Day Three Outline

Minilesson: A string of related problems

❖ Have students count around a circle by 10s, examine and reflect on patterns, and then repeat but skipcounting by 9 this time. Discussion occurs on the resulting patterns in the multiples of 9: the units decrease by one each time; the number of tens increases by one; and the sum of the digits is always 9.

Developing the Context

❖ Mystery #2 is introduced with a story about a secret agent #9 and a meeting, which he has invited several other agents to for a discussion on secret codes.

❖ Send students off in pairs to determine if all the agents have codes that will get them into the meeting, and if so what their codes are.

Supporting the Investigation

❖ As students work, encourage them to draw number lines and build databases to look for patterns in the multiples, and to investigate the sum of the digits as they did in the minilesson.

❖ Confer with pairs as they work, suggesting the use of the base ten blocks where helpful to figure out why the patterns occur.

Math Journals

❖ Provide quiet time for students to write about the things they have noticed and to reflect.

Minilesson: A count-around

Have students sit in a circle in the meeting area. Start them with counting by tens and recording on a ratio table the multiples as they are said, as shown below on the left. After you've gone all the way around the circle invite discussion on the patterns. Students will likely say, "a zero is just being added." Ask if addition of a zero is happening, or if the numeral is being moved over a place to reflect the number of tens.

X10

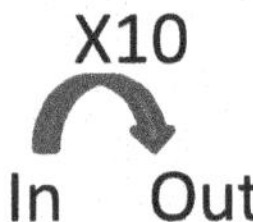

In	Out
1	10
2	20
3	30
4	40
5	50
6	60
7	70
8	80
9	90
10	100
11	110
12	120
25	250

x9

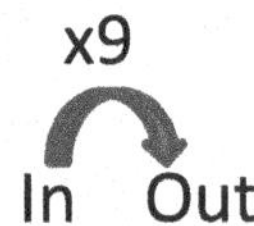

In	Out
1	9
2	18
3	27
4	36
5	45
6	54
7	63
8	72
9	81
10	90
11	99
12	108
25	225

Math Note:

Multiplying by ten is a nice review of some ideas about place value that students may have forgotten, or perhaps never constructed. For example, everything left of the unit column reflects the number of tens in the number. When the 11th person says 110, there are 11 tens in the number. Help students realize this in the discussion. During the discussion encourage them to see 110, not as just 1 hundred, 1 ten, and 0 units, but as 11 tens. Support conversation on the commutative property as a way to justify

As you move on to discussing patterns in the multiples of 9, encourage students to compare the two tables. The prior discussion on the tens will likely support students to realize that when adding nines, the number of tens is increasing by one, but the number of units is decreasing by one. This is because adding nine is equivalent to adding 10-1. And, if a ten is being added but a unit is being removed, the sum of the digits stays the same. Even when one gets to 99, the sum of the digits is 18, but add again: 1 + 8 = 9. And now the divisibility rule is apparent: if the sum of the digits of a number equals 9, the number is divisible by 9—put another way, 9 is a factor of the number. The formal proof of the divisibility rule is to think about 1 missing out of every power of ten when the maximum number of 9s are removed. If the ones remaining when added make another group of 9, the number itself is divisible by 9. The reason base ten blocks are provided as a manipulative tool is to support students, potentially, to see this connection.

Inside One Classroom: A Portion of the Minilesson

Camille (the teacher): Ok, everybody has said a number. Let's step back now and look at what we have. Does anyone see anything interesting and maybe have a way to explain why it is occurring? **Natasha:** You just add a zero when you multiply by ten. **Camille:** Hmmm...When I add 0 to 11, I get 11, not 110. What do you mean by "adding a zero?"	 *Author's notes*
Natasha: Well I don't mean adding like that. The zero goes on the end. **Camille:** And how many tens are in 110? **Natasha:** 1. **Camille:** Only 1? **Ricardo:** No, there are 10 tens in a hundred, too. There are 11 tens in 110. And 12 tens in 120. That's why the 0 goes on the end. To push the numbers over to be tens. **Camille:** What will the next one be then, Natasha? **Natasha:** Oh yeah, I get it...130. It has 13 tens. **Camille:** Interesting, right? 10 is an interesting number in our system. Let's see what happens with 9. Let's count around again by nines. (*As students provide the multiples, Camille makes a new ratio table and records the results*). Ok, we are done. Turn and talk to a partner. Anything interesting to notice here? (*After a few minutes of pair talk, Camille starts whole group discussion*). Juan? **Juan:** The tens are going up again each time, but the ones are going down. **Camille:** Hmmm. So, what's going on here? **Sue:** We think it's because we are adding a ten...so the tens are going up by one. But we're not really adding a ten, we're adding nine, so we have to take away one. **Sydney:** Yep. We agree, and we noticed something else so weird! It starts with 9, right? And then the next one is 18. If you add 1+8 that is 9 again. And then 27 and 2+7 is 9 again. It keeps doing that.	*Camille starts with the tens. Note how she deals with Natasha's comment about adding a zero.* *Camille returns to Natasha to see if she has followed Ricardo's argument.* *Since everyone appears to understand Ricardo's justification, Camille moves the discussion to the next table—the nines. Mathematicians look for structure and regularity—one of the standards of mathematical practice. Camille models this practice.* *Note how Camille invites inquiry.* *Sydney has noticed an important thing. The sum of the digits adds to 9.*

Camille: Whoa! That's an interesting noticing. What's going on there? **Sydney:** Well, we think if you keep adding 1 ten and subtracting 1 unit, the total stays the same. It started at 9 and so it will always be 9. **Camille:** Wow. You are saying a big thing there, I think. Are you suggesting that if the sum of the digits adds up to 9, the number is divisible by 9? Did anyone else think about this? This is big. Turn and talk about this with a partner.	*Notice how Camille compliments and makes the noticing of "big things" feel so special.*

Developing the Context

At the end of the minilesson most students will have noticed and discussed patterns that occur when multiplying by 10 and by 9. The discussion in the minilesson should flow very nicely into the development of the context—mystery #2. Ask students to move and sit with their detective partner from the prior days. Distribute or display Appendix C and tell the story about the meeting for secret agents being held inside the trunk of an old giant redwood tree.

Agent #9 has organized a meeting for a group of secret agents at location 90 *, inside the trunk of an old giant redwood tree in the woods. The purpose of the meeting is for all the agents to share their secret codes and then write them down and bury them together at the location. All agents must use their codes to get to the meeting location.*

Agent #9 chose this spot because he can get there easily. All he needs to do is take 10 steps of 9 along the path and he is there! His secret code is that the sum of the digits must be 9. The location is 90 and he sees right away that his code works, 9+0 =9. He writes it down and explains why his code works, and now he is ready for the meeting.

Remind students of the discussion in the minilesson about how the number of tens was going up by one, and the number of units was going down by one. Using the base ten blocks, lay out 9 tens (sticks) and write the number 90 down on an open number line to model the pathway to the location. Invite students to find the 10 nines in the 9 tens and discuss what agent #9 knows about his code. After a few minutes of pair talk, support a discussion to help students see that in every stick of ten there will be one unit remaining. Draw the 9 jumps of 9 on the open number line. The remainders of 1 in each 10 also make a group of 9 and so 90 is divisible by 9. It can be thought of as 9 nines + 1 group of 9 more and that equals 10 nines.

Draw the last jump on the line. The sum of the digits equals 9, and 90 can also be thought of as 9 tens. Point out the ratio table you filled out in the minilesson and note that the secret code for agent #9 is that the digits in a number have to add up to 9 for the number to be divisible by 9. Then go on with the story.

X9

1	9
2	18
3	27
4	36
5	45
6	54
7	63
8	72
9	81
10	90

Agents #2, #3, #4, #5, #6, and #10 all get the message about the meeting. They wonder, "Will they all be able to get in? Will their secret codes get them to location 90?"

Many students, precisely because of the minilesson and the prior discussion, will immediately say #10 can land on 90 because they know that 10x9 = 9x10. Congratulate them on the use of the commutative property. They also have the 9 tens (sticks) to look at. If you place the sticks in a rectangular array and rotate it 90° you can help them visualize how 9x10 = 10x9. Remind them that numbers that are divisible by 10 end in 0 and this is the code that agent #10 must write down.

Don't let them discuss any more of the agents' codes right now even if they are bursting with ideas! Instead, tell them to work with their partner to determine all the others. Explain that once they know an agent's secret code, they should write it down and be ready to present evidence of their solution for each. And, they should work to determine if all the agents can land on location 90, assuming they can take jumps of their own number only.

Supporting the Investigation

Move around the room as students work, listening and noting the strategies they are using. Remind them that they can draw the pathways for the other agents and see where their steps take them. Suggest they look for common landing spots in case some of the codes are related. Invite them to make databases to help. Then, as always, sit and confer with a few pairs.

Inside One Classroom: Conferring with Students at Work

Camille (the teacher): I've been watching what you two are doing and it looks like such an interesting strategy. May I sit and confer with you? It looks as if you are exploring how the paths of #3 and #9 are related?

Zeke: Yes. We figured out that agent #3 must be a buddy of #9 because #3 keeps meeting up with him, landing on some of the same spots. See, 9....18......27.

Alana: But #3 goes in smaller steps: 3, 6, 9, 12, 15, 18, 21....

Author's notes

Note how Camille listens first before she sits down. She then explains what she thinks the pair is doing and asks for clarification.

Zeke: Right, but 9 and 18 are in there, see? **Camille:** So, you've drawn the pathway and you are marking each step and where they meet? **Zeke:** Yes, we wanted to be sure. We think #9 is going to land on every third one. **Alana:** Because 3x3 = 9. **Camille:** Tell me more about that, Alana. **Alana:** Well, like 3, 6, 9. Nine is the third number and it took 3 steps to get there. 3 threes make 1 nine. Then 12, 15, 18. Both land on 18. Then I added the digits like we noticed in the minilesson. And it's cool. It keeps going 3, 6, 9, 3, 6, 9. **Camille:** *(After some wait time)* Can you see what she's saying, Zeke? **Zeke:** Oh. That's a good idea, Alana. 21.... So, 2+1, that's 3. And 24, 2+4=6. Weird! Wow!	*Once she is sure of their strategy she will be able to better support them. The intent is not to lead them to a strategy she may know, but to support them as young mathematicians to develop their ideas further.* *Notice how Camille encourages Alana to expand. Doing so brings more thinking out and then Camille makes a move to ensure Jake is following.*
Camille: Hmm...Using the base blocks for nine earlier helped us see the leftovers. Let's use them again and see if we can find the threes, and the leftovers. (*She lays out 2 sticks*). **Alana:** There's 7 leftovers in each because 3+7=10. **Camille:** Perhaps we should take out as many threes as we can out of each? **Alana:** What do you mean? **Camille:** Well didn't you say that 3 threes were in nine? So, if we think of the stick that way, there is only 1 leftover. What numbers worked for 3? 20 is not in your list. Is 21 on your list for agent #3? **Zeke:** Yes. **Camille:** Ok, let's add 1 little cube then. So now we have 21. Right? 2 tens, plus 1? When we add 2+1 and get 3, where is it coming from? **Alana:** Oh.....oh.....oh! I think I get it Zeke! It *is* just like #9! There are 3 in every stick and just 1 leftover. So, if the leftovers make 3, 6, or 9, it	*Teachers in my workshops often ask me, "Should we use manipulatives with students?" This is the wrong question to ask. We should be asking, "What would be the benefit of providing a manipulative here, which one, and why?" Encouraging the use of base ten blocks here is a critical, important move by Camille. They were used prior to generate a divisibility rule for 9. The structure of the manipulative will support the emergence now of the divisibility rule for 3, just as it did for 9. Camille wants to help Alana and Jake see a connection.* *Note how Camille at this moment offers a possible direction. This is what good mentors do. Ownership is critical though; it needs to stay with the mathematicians. She doesn't give them a directive; she offers a possibility. The students still get to decide if they want to go in that direction. Camille offers a little more guidance here, still the*

works! See, 21....there is just 1 here so 2+1=3. If we had 24, that would be 2 sticks and 4, so REALLY two leftovers and 4. That's 6. Two more groups of 3. And 27 has 2 leftovers and 7. That's 9, 3 more groups of 3.	*ownership remains with the young mathematicians, though. And now the insight comes!*
Camille: Wow! This is big! I think you are cracking agent #3's code! I wonder if agent #6's code is related, too. Could you take this investigation even further? What do you think? What spots does #6 land on? You could try making databases for 3, 6, and 9 and see if they are related. I'll check back with you later, ok? I need to go confer with a few other kids. Wow. This is so exciting!	*Camille challenges them with finding a divisibility rule for 6, and then leaves to allow them sufficient time to work through their thinking.*

Math Note:

Most students will remember a divisibility rule for #2, and possibly #4, from the work done on the prior 2 days. A data base for #2 is important here, though, for a comparison with multiples of #6. Because 6 has 2 groups of 3 in it, its rule is the same as the rule for 3, except for one big exception. Only even numbers work, because 6 has 2 threes in it. 21 is odd and not divisible by 6, although it is divisible by three. 24 is even and thus is divisible by both 6 and 3.

As students work they will likely also start noticing that some of the multiples of 10 are found in the databases of #2 and #5. The code for #5 is that its multiples must end in 5 or 0. Multiples of 2, end in 0, 2, 4, 6, 8. And tens end only in 0. The factors of 10 are 2 and 5. Two groups of 5 are needed to make a 10.

As math workshop begins to draw to a close, provide students with quiet reflection time to write in their journals. Tomorrow they will have an opportunity to work further, to write the codes up on sticky notes to be buried inside the tree trunk, and to prepare justifications on posters for a gallery walk and congress. In this investigation, it is not important that every student crack every agent's code. What is important is that they enjoy the mystery, and that each individual student gets as far with the "codes" as he or she can.

Reflections on the Day

Today your students had the opportunity to examine the beautiful patterns in our base-ten number system that occur when multiplying. Tomorrow students will have an opportunity to revisit what they discovered by reading back over the notes they wrote in their journals today. They will have more time to work if needed and then they will prepare posters of their findings for a gallery walk and congress on Day Four. Note the division strategies students are using as this provides you with important information to inform your choices as you do further minilessons with your group over the course of the next few weeks. Celebrate their noticings and how they justify their thinking. Remember to reflect on what you see each day, on the big ideas being constructed, and on the strategies that you see being used. Document the growth you see on the landscape. If you are using the New Perspectives assessment app, take a short video clip and a picture of children's work and add it to the landscape.

DAY FOUR

DIVISIBILITY RULES

Materials Needed

Students' work from Day Three

Lined Sticky Notes, four to six per student

Math Journals

Markers and Pencils

Today begins with a minilesson using a string of related problems designed to support the development of division strategies. After the minilesson, students review their journal notes, and then either finish working or begin a poster on their findings in preparation for a gallery walk, where they notice and wonder about other students' findings and compare them to their own. After the gallery walk, a math congress is held to discuss a few of the emerging ideas about divisibility rules. The day ends with journal writing.

Day Four Outline

Minilesson: A String of Related Problems

❖ Work on a string of related division problems to encourage further discussion on divisibility rules and strategies for division.

Facilitating the Gallery Walk

❖ Confer with children as they finish up work and put finishing touches on their posters asking them to consider the most important things they want to tell their audience.

❖ Conduct a gallery walk to allow students time to reflect and comment on each other's posters.

Facilitating the Math Congress

❖ Convene students at the meeting area to discuss a few important ideas about divisibility rules that have surfaced in their work.

Math Journals

❖ At the end of the congress, provide everyone with some reflective writing time.

Minilesson: A String of Related Problems

Work through each problem one at a time inviting students to share their strategies. Use the open number line to represent students' thinking as jumps, as they will likely see connections to the steps of the agents they have been investigating. For example, the first problem can be represented as 30 steps of 2 (or as half of 60, as 2 groups of 30). Invite discussion on agent #2 and the landing spots to help students connect the investigation, which they are in the midst of, to the minilesson.

The String:

60 / 2

60 / 4

62 / 2

62 / 4

64 / 4

100 / 4

200 / 4

164 / 4

264 / 4

224 / 4

Behind the Numbers

This string has been carefully constructed to support students' understanding of how division by 2 and by 4 are related, and also to potentially support some discussion (or review if it was discussed on Day Two) on a divisibility rule for 4: since 100 is divisible by 4, any number of hundreds also is divisible by 4. Therefore, one only needs to look at the tens and ones. If that number is also divisible by 4, then the whole number is. For example, note the last four problems in the string. The last problem in the string makes use of 200/4. Since 200 is divisible by 4, and since 24 is divisible by 4 also, the whole number is divisible by 4. An equation to represent this idea is, 224/4 = 200/4 + 24/4, and the related strategy and big idea on the landscape respectively are "using partial quotients" and "the generalized use of the distributive property of multiplication for division."

The numbers are kept small to allow you to go through the string fairly quickly. Focus discussion on the relationships that students see between the problems, rather than on a variety of strategies to get the answer to an individual problem. Providing the minilesson at this point is purposeful. You may find that some of your students notice relationships that bring them to comment on a code for agent #4. Suggest they add their insight as they prepare posters for the subsequent gallery walk and congress. Even if it was discussed in the congress on Day Two, not all students may have understood it. This minilesson provides another opportunity for discussion of it.

Facilitating the Gallery Walk

Ask students to meet in small review groups (usually comprised of 2 pairs of students), with their journals, and to begin by reading over their journal notes from yesterday. Provide 5 minutes of quiet time for them to do so and then provide discussion time. As students discuss common meeting points of the agents, and the various "codes" of the agents and their justifications for them, move around and listen in to a few of the conversations. Doing so will help you confer when postering begins shortly for the gallery walk. After about 10 minutes, have students begin making posters (one for each peer review group) and, as they work, move around and confer. Look for ways to take students' understanding to a deeper level by helping them to justify and generalize their observations and conjectures. As the teacher, you are a mentor. But, you are also a member of the audience. Asking questions will help students clarify their ideas. For example, try out some of the following questions:

- "What do you want me to understand about what you found out? Can you justify it in a way that convinces me?"
- "How do you think your fellow mathematicians will make sense of your ideas?"
- "What do you know with certainty, and what still puzzles you?"

Remind students that it is not necessary to write about everything they did. The posters are not necessarily explanations of everything that was done (false starts, mistakes, and changes made), but instead are justifications of steps for a complete solution, viable arguments of generalizations, or proofs of conjectures and insights. By providing postering time and a gallery walk, you are providing students with an important opportunity to review and refine their thinking—to read and write a viable mathematical argument. This is one of the standards of mathematical practice and an important purpose of the gallery walk.

Once students have posted their work, remind them that gallery walks should be quiet times so that all mathematicians can read and think before commenting. As mentioned previously, this time should be taken seriously. Distribute the sticky notes to students and take some yourself, as well. During the gallery walk you can comment on a few posters, but it's important for you, as well, to look at all the pieces for big ideas and strategies from the landscape so you can plan which pieces of work you will select for the congress.

Facilitating the Math Congress

Review the posters and choose a few that you can use for a discussion that will deepen understanding and support growth along the landscape of learning described in the Overview. In particular, look for posters that provide a way to focus conversation on the following topics:

- all agents except #4 can meet at the location point. #4 can meet at location 88 and 92, but not 90. The earlier minilesson should be helpful in providing some nice insights into why this is.
- common meeting points (common multiples) and why they occur
- patterns in the sequences (for example that all multiples of 6, 10, 4, and 2 are even) and why they occur, including a discussion on prime factorization if the potential for it comes up

- the agents' "codes" (divisibility rules) and their justifications

A window into one classroom during the math congress follows:

Inside One Classroom: A Portion of the Math Congress

Author's notes

Camille (the teacher): Let's start with you, Rafael and Carolina. You noticed an interesting thing in the sequences of the numbers. Come tell us about it.

Camille starts the congress with a discussion on patterns that have been noticed in the sequences. Doing so will provide a nice foundation for a discussion on operations with odd and even numbers, the commutative property, and factorization.

Rafael: Yes. This is so cool. First we thought that it would only be #2 that would land on numbers ending in 0, 2, 4, 6, and 8, because those numbers would be even and #2 can only land on even numbers. But then we noticed that the landing points for #4, #6, and #10 were all even, too!

Carolina: Right. No odd numbers at all, and we don't know why. See… 6, 12, 18, 24, 30, 36, 42, all even and they end in 0, 2, 4, 6, and 8, just like #2. But #3, #5, and #9 all land on both even and odd numbers and #6 is related to #3. It is every other group of 3—2 groups of 3, #3 just goes in smaller steps: 3, 6, 9, 12, 15, 18, 21….

Rafael: But the sixes are in there, every other one, see…? So why does #6 have a sequence sort of like #2?

Camille: What an interesting thing to notice! Let's all turn to an elbow partner and talk about this. Why are these patterns happening? (*After a few minutes of pair talk, Camille resumes whole group discussion*). Maia?

Notice how Camille turns the conversation into pair talk at this moment? Doing so provides needed reflection time on some underlying big ideas and will enable more engagement in the conversation she will pursue next.

Maia: Maybe because 6 has a 2 in it?

Camille: Tell us more about that, Maia.

Maia: Well, like 3, 6, 9,12, 15, 18, 21. It goes odd, even, odd, even. 6 is 2x3. So, it skips a number every time. #4 and #2 were related like that also. #4 landed on every other number that #2 landed on.

Camille: *(After some wait time)* Can you see what she's saying, Rafael and Carolina?

Rafael: Yes, I see why it is like #3. But why is it like the sequence of #2?

Rafael has asked a poignant question and Camille provides more pair talk.

Camille: Hmm…good question. (*Camille makes two ratio tables: one for the function x3, recording 3, 6, 9, 12, 15, 18; the other for the function x2, recording 2, 4, 6, 8, 10, 12, 15, 18.*) Ok, let's turn and talk again with a partner.	
Carolina: There's 2x3 there (*pointing to the sequence made by x3, and there is 3x2 there (pointing to the sequence made by x3*). I get it! Maia is right! 6 has 2 and 3 in it!	Note how Camille at this moment offers a counter example to foster puzzlement. Doing so pushes her students to examine the multiplicative structuring.
Camille: But 5 has a 2 and 3 in it, too. 2+3 is 5. Why doesn't it happen with 5? What is different? #5 goes 5, 10, 15, 20, 25… (*Several students now look very puzzled*).	
Carolina: That is addition 2 + 3 = 5. This is multiplication. 2 *times* 3. That means 3 + 3. Oh! I just saw something else, too! 10 = 2 x 5. So, #10 has to have only even landing spots, just like #6. That's why all its landing spots end in 0. #5's spots go odd, even, odd, even, but #10's spots have to be even because there is a 2 in 10.	And now the insight comes!
Camille: Oh! And you don't mean 2 + 8 because that is addition? It's not about addends; it's about factors?	
Zeke: Yes. I get it now, too!	
Camille: Let's look at 9. Did #9 have any even landing spots?	
Alana: Oh…..oh…..oh, no. Yes. #9 is 3x3, but it landed on 18. No even factors, but when it is multiplied by an even number it gets one!	Notice how Camille shows excitement regarding mathematical puzzles and inquiries. She is not only modeling what drives mathematicians—the search for structure and regularity—she is modeling enjoyment in the puzzlement of not knowing.
Camille: Wow! This is big! So, the only factors that 9 has are 1, 3, and 9? Only 3 factors and all odd numbers? Why does it land sometimes on even numbers? Here's its sequence: 9, 18, 27, 36, 45… Every other one is even. This is so exciting! What a puzzle!	
Alana: Maybe when it is multiplied by an even number? 2x9, 4x9, 6x9?	
Camille: Oh, so 9x2 has to be even, (*Camille writes, 2, 4, 6, 8, 10, 12, 14, 16, **18***) and 2x9 has to be even (*writing 9, **18**, 27, 36…*)?	The commutative property now comes forth. Both expressions have a factor of 2.
Rafael: Yes, because 9x2=2x9.	

Math Journals

At the end of the congress, provide everyone with some individual reflective writing time. Questions you might ask students to address are:

- Did you hear about an idea in math workshop that you thought was interesting or particularly powerful?
- Is there a new idea that you are now thinking about? How will you start investigating it?

Reflections on the Day

Today your students had the opportunity to further deepen their understanding of our number system. As they explore sequences of multiples and notice common multiples in the search for structure and regularity, new questions emerge about common factors, and prime factorization. Today you also had another chance to look at your students' work and get a better idea of where each student is travelling on the landscape of learning. Remember to track each student's mathematical development on individual landscapes! Tomorrow they will travel further into the wilderness and wonders of the number system as they begin exploring the geometric shapes numbers!

DAY FIVE

SQUARES AND CUBES

Materials Needed

Approximately 100 Multilink cubes per pair

Graph paper

Math Journals

Pencils

Mystery #3
(Appendix D, one per pair of students)

Today begins with another minilesson on division, this time using divisibility rules when the divisors are prime and exploring what happens to the quotient when the divisors are doubled. Then a new investigation is introduced which involves students further with prime factors, but also extends it to an exploration of square and cubic numbers and their geometric shapes.

Day Five Outline

Minilesson: a string of related problems

❖ Work on a string of related problems designed to encourage the use of divisibility rules when the divisor is a prime number and to understand what happens to the quotient when the divisor is doubled.

Developing the Context

❖ Explain that over the next several days the class will engage in exploring how some of the secret agents can transform into shapes. Today, the mystery to crack is which agents can transform into squares or cubes, and are there some numbers that can do both?

❖ Students build sequences for square numbers and sequences for cubic numbers.

Supporting the Investigation

❖ Note students' strategies as they work and encourage them to use the graph paper to explore square numbers, and to build cube numbers with multilink cubes if they are not sure of a possible transformation. Support them to make sequences for square numbers and cube numbers, and then to use the sequences to predict others.

Minilesson: A String of Related Problems

Do one expression at a time, asking students first, "Will there be a remainder, or not, and how do you know?" Facilitate discussion on this question, thereby promoting a focus and reminder of some of the ideas that have emerged on prior days, and then request the quotient and strategies used to get it. Represent students' strategies as they share using an open array. For example, if a student solves 132/2 as 100/2 + 30/2 + 2/2, draw the following representation:

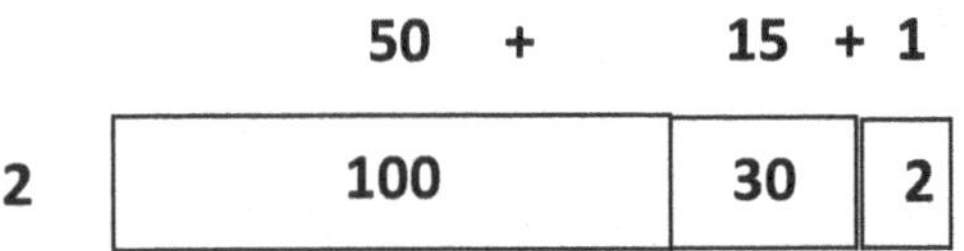

When there is a remainder, for example as in the case of 146/4, you can make a 4 x 36 array and add on just ½ of another column.

The String

132/2
132/4
146/2
146/4
144/4
33/3
33/6
36/6
132/3
132/6
160/10
160/5

Behind the Numbers

The numbers (and the question) have been chosen carefully to support students to *use* the divisibility rules that most likely have emerged over the prior two days. The first several dividends are divisible by 2, but not always by 4. When the divisor doubles, the quotient halves. Halving the quotient of 73 from the third problem to do the fourth (146/4), produces a fraction, which makes sense because 146 is not divisible by 4 without a remainder occurring. Some students may remember the divisibility rule for 4: that any number of hundreds works, but the last two digits must be divisible by 4 as well. 100/4 works but 46/4 does not. The next 5 problems are designed to explore division by 3 and by 6. The sum of the digits in 33 is 6, so division by 3 works, but 33 is not even so division by 6 without a remainder does not. In the last two problems, division by 10 is likely easy. If not, remind students to just note that the answer can be seen in the number if place value is used. 160 has 16 tens in it. 160/5 should now also be easy if students realize that since the divisor has been halved, the quotient from the prior problem, 16, can just be doubled. Encourage students to use these number relations when they divide. This is what numeracy is about!

Developing the Context

Display Appendix D and inform students that there is another mystery for the detectives to crack.

The secret agents have learned that their codes have been cracked and so at some locations they have started to transform themselves into shapes. For example, when 2 arrives on 4, she transforms herself into a square, and when she arrives on 8, she transforms herself into a cube.

2x2 = 4

2x2x2 = 8

The agents all start making two sequences: one for square numbers; and one for cube numbers.

This is what they have so far:

1, 4, 9, 16, 25.....

1, 8, 27, 64, 125....

Which sequence is which? And, what comes next in these sequences? Are there any numbers that can be a square and a cube?

Pass out Appendix D, one copy per pair of students. Provide Multilink Cubes and graph paper as tools, as many students may want (and need) to make the shapes to be convinced. Send them off in pairs to work on the questions on Appendix D.

Supporting the Investigation

Move around and confer as students work. You may note some of the following strategies:

- Some students may start by drawing squares using the graph paper. This is a nice way to start because then they can also explore the increasing differences in the sequence. The difference between 1 and 4 is 3; the difference between 4 and 9 is 5; the difference between 9 and 16 is 7. The difference of consecutive squares is a sequence of odd numbers! This is happening because an L shaped piece is being added to each prior square each time, comprised of a new row, a new column, plus 1 extra square for the new corner. As you confer, you can encourage students to note some of these relations and wonder about them.
- Some students may think of the squares as an area. As you confer, you can support them to notice how the area of the square changes in relation to the dimensions: when the dimension is doubled, the area increases by a factor of 2^2. When the dimensions are tripled, the area increases by a factor of 3^2. Encourage students to use graph paper to explore this.
- When students explore the cube numbers, many students will build them with Multilink Cubes. As you confer, support students to notice how the cubes relate to volume. When the dimensions double, the volume increases by a factor of 2^3. When the dimensions are tripled, the volume increases by a factor of 3^3.
- As the numbers become larger, students may start having difficulty with the arithmetic and may begin making a lot of mistakes as they calculate. At this point it may be helpful to provide calculators. But, be careful not to provide them too soon as students may just use them to derive answers and may not explore the resulting patterns.
- When students begin to find numbers that are in both sequences (for example, 64), encourage them to write down where they came from. In the example of 64, it is 8x8 (a square), but it is also 4x4x4 (a cube). Support students to see the 2s and how the associative property is involved:

$$(2x2x2) \text{ x } (2x2x2) = (2x2) \text{ x } (2x2) \text{ x } (2x2)$$

As math workshop begins to draw to a close, provide students with quiet reflection time to write in their journals. Tomorrow they will have an opportunity to work further and to prepare a poster for a gallery walk and congress.

Reflection on the Day

Today provided students with a chance to explore how numbers can be thought of as shapes—specifically, as squares and cubes. As the unit continues, there will be multiple opportunities for students to explore several other sequences that can also be represented with shapes—primes, composites, and triangular numbers. You are making the standards of mathematical practice come alive. Your students are structuring and examining regularities. They are exploring patterns, raising conjectures, and working to prove them. Be proud of your young mathematicians, and yourself for offering them opportunities to do so!

DAY SIX

PRIMES AND COMPOSITES

Materials Needed

Students' work from Day Five

Lined Sticky Notes, four to six per student

Math Journals

Markers and Pencils

Today begins with a minilesson, *Transform Me*. Students are asked to transform numbers into rectangles. Generating the shape of the number also generates the factors and students learn to distinguish primes, composites, squares, and cubes. After the minilesson, students review their journal notes from Day Five, and then either finish working or begin a poster on their findings in preparation for a gallery walk, where they notice and wonder about other students' findings and compare them to their own. After the gallery walk, a math congress is held to discuss a few of the emerging ideas about factors, multiples, and the shapes of numbers.

Day Six Outline

Minilesson: Transform Me

❖ Work on a string of related numbers to explore factors and the shapes of numbers to encourage discussion on primes, composites, squares, and cubes.

Facilitating the Gallery Walk

❖ Confer with children as they finish up work and put finishing touches on their posters, asking them to consider the most important things they want to tell their audience.

❖ Conduct a gallery walk to allow students time to reflect and comment on each other's posters.

Facilitating the Math Congress

❖ Convene students at the meeting area to discuss a few important ideas about factors and multiples that have surfaced in their work.

Minilesson: A String of Related Problems

Present the numbers in the string one at a time, inviting students to imagine the number being transformed into rectangles. With each response, invite discussion on the shape and the dimensions, generating as many rectangles as possible, and listing the factors (the dimensions of each rectangle). Use the open array to represent students' thinking. For example, the first number in the string is 36. Students might imagine this number as 1 x 36, 2 x 18, 3 x 12, 4 x 9, or 6 x 6. As they put forth ideas draw each rectangle, transforming one rectangle into another as new ideas are put forth and listing the factors for each. For example, a 1x32 rectangle can be cut in half to form two 1x18 rectangles. When these smaller rectangles are moved and placed one above the other, a 2x18 results. If the 1x36 is cut into three parts, each will be 1x12. When repositioned the new rectangle is now a 3x12. Mark a chart with two categories, labeling one *primes* and the other *composites.* After the rectangles are determined, place the number in the appropriate category, noting that numbers that only have 2 factors (1 and itself) are called primes, and numbers that can transform into more than one rectangle are called composites—thus 2, 13, 3, 5, and 7 are primes and all the others are composites. Note that 36 is a composite, although it is also a square!

The String:

36

2

18

15

13

3

5

7

6

Math Note:

A prime number (or a prime) is a natural number greater than 1 that has no positive divisors other than 1 and itself. A natural number greater than 1 that is not a prime number is called a composite number. For example, 5 is prime because 1 and 5 are its only positive integer factors, whereas 6 is a composite because it has the divisors 2 and 3 in addition to 1 and 6. Square and cube numbers are also composite numbers as they have more than 2 factors. The number 1 is not a prime or composite because it has only 1 factor.

Facilitating the Gallery Walk

Ask students to look back over the notes they made in their journals at the end of Day Five and to finish up their work. As they finish, move them into postering. Move around and confer as they work, looking for ways to take students' understanding to a deeper level by helping them to justify and generalize their observations and conjectures.

Once students have posted their work, remind them that gallery walks should be quiet times so that all mathematicians can read and think before commenting. Distribute the sticky notes to students and take some yourself, as well.

Facilitating the Math Congress

Review the posters and choose a few that you can use for a discussion that will deepen understanding and support growth along the landscape of learning described in the Overview. In particular, look for posters that provide a way to focus conversation on the following topics:

- If you have some students that have drawn out the squares on graph paper this is a nice place to start, particularly if they have also explored the increasing differences in the sequence. Focus conversation on the differences and why they occur. The difference of consecutive squares is a sequence of odd numbers. This is happening because an L shaped piece is being added to each prior square each time, comprised of a new row, a new column, plus 1 extra square for the new corner.
- If you have some students that discussed area and noted how the area of the square changes in relation to the dimensions, this is a nice piece to use next. Focus the discussion on what happens to the area when the dimensions double, or triple.
- End with a piece that allows for a discussion on the sequences for the squares and cubes: 1,4,9,16,25,36,49,64..... and 1,8,27,64,125... and focus the discussion on how both 1 and 64 can be both a square and a cube. Provide time to discuss the dimensions and how the shapes were formed. In the example of 64, it is 8x8 (a square), but it is also 4x4x4 (a cube). Support students to see the 2s and how the associative property is involved:

$$(2 \times 2 \times 2) \times (2 \times 2 \times 2) = (2 \times 2) \times (2 \times 2) \times (2 \times 2)$$

Math Note:

It is not likely that your student will find other numbers besides 1 and 64 that can be both, and it is not important that they do so. It is more the intrigue and the mystery that you want to foster. But you might be interested to note that 2^6 allows for groupings into 2 factors and 3 factors. Therefore, another number that will also work is 3^6 because it can be formed into (3x3x3)x(3x3x3) to make a 27x27 square, and into (3x3)x(3x3)x(3x3) to make a 9x9x9 cube. Any prime number raised to the 6th power is a square and a cube.

Math Journals

At the end of the congress, provide everyone with some individual reflective writing time. Questions you might ask students to address are:

- Did you hear about an idea in math workshop that you thought was interesting or particularly powerful?
- Is there a new idea that you are now thinking about? How will you start investigating it?

Reflections on the Day

Today your students had the opportunity to further deepen their understanding of our number system by exploring primes, composites, squares and cubes. Tomorrow they will work further with primes and composites and try to determine if there is any way to determine how many factors a number has without needing to draw all the rectangular arrays.

DAY SEVEN

HOW MANY FACTORS DOES A NUMBER HAVE?

Materials Needed

Appendix E (sorting numbers by the number of factors they have), 1 copy per pair of students.

Drawing Paper

Graph paper

Math Journals

Pencils

Today begins with another *Transform Me* minilesson (similar to the one on the prior day) to provide a continuation of the work on distinguishing primes and composites and students are again asked to transform numbers into rectangles to generate the factors. After the minilesson, a new mystery is introduced. Students collect data on the number of factors a number has and investigate if there is any way to know how many factors a number has without needing to make all the arrays.

Day Seven Outline

Minilesson: Transform Me

❖ Work on a string of related numbers to encourage more discussion on primes and composites.

Developing the Context

❖ Reflect back on the minilesson. Wonder aloud if there might be a way to tell ahead how many factors a number has without having to draw all the arrays. Suggest that pairs of detectives investigate this and perhaps begin by sorting numbers by the number of factors they each have to see if there are any patterns.

❖ Display Appendix E, sorting a few numbers to get students started, and then send them off to work.

Supporting the Investigation

❖ Note students' strategies as they work and move around and confer. If students have difficulty thinking of all the factors, remind them to draw arrays to see if there are ways to transform them to find other factors. Support students to notice that prime numbers squared all have 3 factors and prime numbers cubed all have 4 factors and to investigate why. Invite journal reflections.

Minilesson: A String of Related Problems

Present the numbers in the string one at a time, inviting students to imagine the number being transformed into rectangles. With each response, invite discussion on the shape and the dimensions, generating as many rectangles for each as possible, listing the factors, and filling out a table labeled primes and composites. Use the open array to represent students' thinking. For example, 2 and 3 are primes. Only one rectangle can be drawn for each, a 1x2 and a 1x3. The number 6 however is a composite with 4 factors (1, 2, 3, and 6.) Two rectangles can thus be drawn, a 1x6 and a 2x3. As students put forth ideas, draw each rectangle, transforming one rectangle into another as new ideas are put forth and listing the dimensions (factors) for each. Add to the chart you started yesterday for *primes* and *composites,* reminding students that numbers that have only 2 factors (1 and itself) are called primes, and numbers that have more than 2 factors are called composites.

The String:

2

3

6

12

5

10

20

15

30

Developing the Context

After the minilesson is over, wonder aloud about how some numbers seem to have a lot of factors and others have very few. Ask students if they think there might be a way to tell how many factors a number has without needing to draw all the arrays. Suggest that this is another mystery for the detectives to crack.

Display Appendix E and suggest that students begin by sorting numbers into piles by the number of factors they have. To get everyone started do a few together. For example, start with 1 and ask how many factors it has. Once students justify that it has only one factor, list it in the category of 1-factor numbers. Next do 2, and 3. Since both are prime they will each have 2 factors, so list them there. 4 has 3 factors (1,2, and 4), so list it under the category 3-factor numbers. Then send students off with Appendix E to continue sorting and to investigate whether there are any patterns, or not.

Supporting the Investigation

Provide everyone with time to start sorting before you sit and confer. Move around and make sure that students are determining the number of factors and not confusing this goal with listing the precise factors. Having several sheets available of both blank and graph paper (or they can work in their journals) is helpful so that they have a place to determine all the factors, draw arrays if needed, and list the factors of each number before they count them. If several students are challenged by sorting this way, stop the work momentarily and do a few more together, filling in more of the sheet until you have something like the display shown in Figure 5. Then send them back to work again and confer as needed to ensure students understand that they are to sort numbers into categories of # of factors a given number has to see if there are any patterns.

1-Factor Numbers	2-Factor Numbers	3-Factor Numbers	4-Factor Numbers	5-Factor Numbers	6-Factor Numbers	7-Factor Numbers	8-Factor Numbers	9-Factor Numbers	10-Factor Numbers
1	2	4	6	16	12				
	3	9	8						
	5		10						
	7		14						
	11		15						
	13								

Figure 5: Numbers 1 through 16 sorted appropriately

Then move around again allowing students to sort further until you hear some interesting conjectures starting to happen. For example, note the student work shown in Figure 6. These students have started adding some more squares into the category of 3-factor numbers. Note that some of the numbers listed do have only 3 factors, but others have more and thus are categorized incorrectly. 47 is also a prime, but the students made a calculation error as they worked on 7x7. However, the important thing to note is that the students have raised a conjecture about square numbers and supporting them to test it and to examine the results should be the focus of a conferral. A sample conferral around this piece of work is shown in the following dialogue box as well.

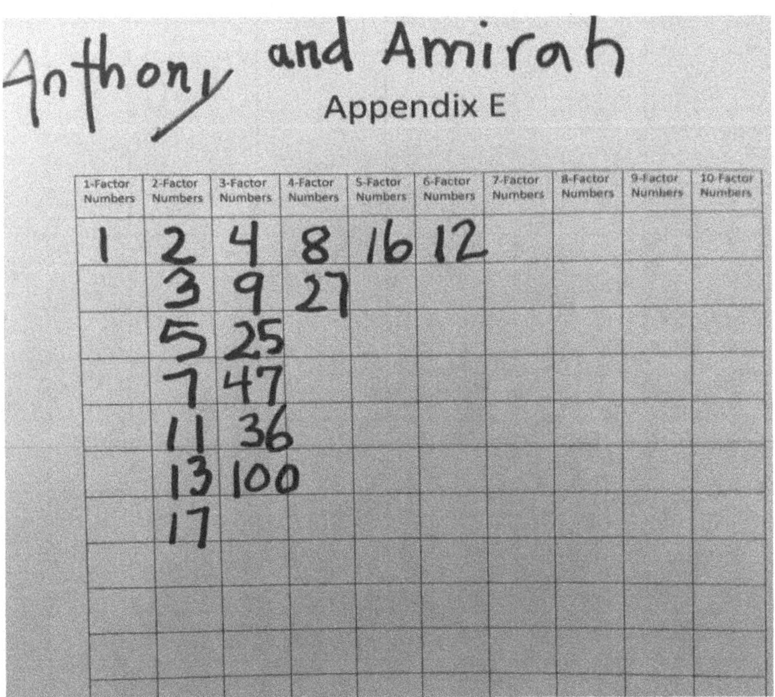
Anthony and Amirah

Appendix E

1-Factor Numbers	2-Factor Numbers	3-Factor Numbers	4-Factor Numbers	5-Factor Numbers	6-Factor Numbers	7-Factor Numbers	8-Factor Numbers	9-Factor Numbers	10-Factor Numbers
1	2	4	8	16	12				
	3	9	27						
	5	25							
	7	47							
	11	36							
	13	100							
	17								

Figure 6: Sample Student Work Being Discussed in the Dialogue Box

Inside One Classroom: Conferring with Students at Work

Camille (the teacher): I've been watching what you two are doing and it looks like you have a conjecture. May I sit and confer with you? It looks as if you are exploring square numbers and you think there might be a pattern?

Anthony: We think maybe the numbers in the third column are the squares. Four is a square number. It is 2x2. And 9 is a square number. It is 3x3.

Camille: Wow! That's a very interesting conjecture! Is that why you also wrote 47, 36, and 100?

Author's notes

Note how Camille listens first before she sits down. She then explains what she thinks the pair is doing and asks for clarification. Once she is sure of their strategy she will be

Amirah: Yes, we know 10x10 is 100. 47 is 7x7 and 36 is 6x6. **Camille:** Wow. Won't this be cool if you are right? How are you going to go about proving this? **Amirah:** We know 4 is right. We did that one and the factors are 1 and 4. We did an array to show people, and then we made one for 2x2. But you can only count the 2 once, see, because it is the same number when it is a square.	*able to better support them. Note also that she does not comment first on their mistakes. Instead, she celebrates their idea and challenges them to justify it. Along the way they will discover their mistakes on their own more naturally.*
Camille: Oh, now that is an interesting piece of information! When it is a square it uses the same factor twice? Did that happen with 9, too? **Anthony:** Yep. See, 1x9 and 3x3. So, the factors are 1, 3, and 9. See? There are only 3 factors. And the same with 25. It's just 1x25 and 5x5.	*Notice how Camille encourages and then supports them to focus on a big idea about squares. The dimensions are the same so even though there are 2 rectangles that can be made, since one is a square, only one factor is gained, not two.*
Camille: Wow! This is very interesting. 2, 3, and 5 were also in your list of primes, too, so I guess they only had 2 factors? And then when you squared it, one more happened? How about the 47? And could you tell me first how you got 47? **Amirah:** We couldn't remember 7x7, but we knew 3x7 was 21, and 21 + 21 is ....42. Then we counted on, 43, 44, 45, 46, ...oh! Anthony we made a mistake. 47, 48, 49! It's 49!	*Note how Camille at this moment subtly offers a possible direction to explain why primes squared are 3-factor numbers. This is what good mentors do—they focus reflection on important ideas. Ownership is critical though; it needs to stay with the mathematicians. She doesn't give them a directive; she clarifies an insight, but she doesn't push it. She also probes about the 47, which will support them to reflect on their error. Rather than correcting their error, she supports them to find it and correct it themselves.*
Camille: That was nice thinking, Amirah. When we forget a fact, it is really a good idea to use one we know and adjust from it instead of having to add up all the 7s. That's what you did. You used 6x7 and counted on. Nice thinking. Ok, so it is 49. Why don't you fix that on your chart? Then let's see if there are only 3 factors. Let's see, we have 1x49. Would 2 work? **Amirah:** No, because it is ending in 9. 2 can only land on 0, 2, 4, 6, and 8, remember? **Camille:** Right, more good thinking. I think we had a rule last week for #3, too, right? Didn't the sum of the digits need to be 3, 6, or 9? And 49....4+9....that is 13, right? Ok 3 is out. What about 4? **Anthony:** Won't work. 4x10 is 40. So, there are 9 left. And 2x4 gets us to 8, so there is a remainder. 4 won't work. And 5 won't because it ends in 9, not 0 or 5. Maybe 6..... Nope, remember 6 was like	*Camille compliments them on the good thinking they did to figure out the square of 7. They have made use of some nice alternative strategies based on a deep understanding of number and operation. By the end of grade 4, it will be nice to have the basic facts automatic, but one can always forget, and having alternative shortcut strategies to fall back on is important. Plus, they are using the properties!*

3 and it had to be even! 49 is not even and it didn't even work for 3, so it won't work for 6. Besides, I know 6x8 is 48, not 49. **Camille:** It is helpful when you just know the fact, isn't it? So, do we need to do anymore? If 6 doesn't work because 6x8 is 48, will 8 work? **Anthony:** (quiet and thinking)...I don't think so because 8x6 is the same as 6x8....it's the "turn around"....it's 48, too. There are only 3 factors, 1, 7, and 49. We're right Amirah!	*Notice how the divisibility rules explored and generated during the first week of this unit are now coming in handy.*
Camille: Hmmmm.... I'm puzzled though. It seems 2, 3, 5, and 7 all worked. The squares of these numbers do all have only 3 factors. But, I'm looking at your 100. You listed it here, too? Doesn't 100 have a lot of factors? 1, 2, 4....4x25, right? So, we need to list 25 also. And there is 50, too, because 2x50... And we haven't even gotten to the square yet....that is 10x10, right? So, let's see....how many is that? 1, 100, 2, 50, 4, 25, 5, 20,...5x20 is 100, too, and 10? Is this 9 factors? Yikes, a lot of factors...not even close to 3! But, it is a square number. Why doesn't 100 work, when the other square numbers you tried all worked? What's different with 10x10? **Amirah:** (looking on the table for 10) We didn't do 10, Anthony. How many factors does 10 have? .....1, 2, 5, and 10. 4 factors. Let's put 10 in the 4-factor column. **Anthony:** Maybe because the others were primes? They only had 2 factors, so when we squared them, it was just 2 plus 1 more?	*Anthony and Amirah are really working on some important ideas here. And now is the time to challenge. Do all square numbers have only 3 factors; or is it only the squares of the primes? What about 100? Camille challenges and ups the ante by offering a counterexample. This is also what good mentors do.*
Camille: Wow! You guys are really thinking hard today about this. I need to get to other kids right now and see how they are doing, too. But, I think you might be on to something very interesting, very big! Keep going and tell me later what you come up, ok? I'm really fascinated by what you are doing. And now you even have me wondering about the cubes of primes!	*There is no need to stay for long periods with students when conferring. The goal is to listen, celebrate, and challenge. And, when you walk away, the students should feel charged and excited to continue.*

Math Note:

Prime numbers are a critical component for students to take note of, as every positive integer (except 1) has primes in it. In years to come your students will be expected to do and understand prime factorization, not just to find factor pairs. Consider 100. It can thought of as $2^2 \times 5^2 = 100$. Since squares of primes have 3 factors each, there will be 9 factors in 100 (found by adding 1 to each exponent and multiplying). It is certainly not expected that 4th graders come to understand prime factorization at this point in their development. The inquiry is offered here only because it is so rich with "high ceiling" opportunities, while also having "low floor opportunities," thus allowing for many entry points with learning opportunities for all. Some children will be challenged just by finding all the factors. Others may notice that squares of primes have one more factor for a total of 3. Natural differentiation is happening, with everyone working on developmentally-appropriate challenges. Don't try to push all your students to see prime factorization, or even to see the same thing. They will go as far as they can go and that is all that is expected. Everyone is learning, but everyone is not likely learning the same thing. Enjoy the insights they have and just celebrate their discoveries! They are young mathematicians at work.

Math Journals

As the end of math workshop draws near, provide everyone with some individual reflective writing time to make notes on what they have discovered thus far, and on what they want to work further on tomorrow.

Reflection on the Day

Today provided students with another chance to explore primes and composites and to consider how many factors different numbers have. As they explore, they are building beautiful structures—a network of number relations and related ideas. Tomorrow, students will have an opportunity to meet first in peer review groups and then will return to work. Posters will be made, and a math congress will ensue.

DAY EIGHT

THE IMPORTANCE OF PRIMES

Today begins with a minilesson using a string of related problems designed to support discussion on factors as divisors. After the minilesson, students form peer review groups and discuss their journal notes from the prior day, and then either finish working or begin a poster on their findings in preparation for a gallery walk. After the gallery walk, a math congress is held to discuss a few of the emerging ideas about the importance of primes. The day ends with journal writing.

Materials Needed

Students' work from Day Seven

Lined Sticky Notes, four to six per student

Chart paper

Math Journals

Markers and Pencils

Day Eight Outline

Minilesson: A String of Related Problems

❖ Work on a string of related multiplication and division problems to encourage discussion on factors as divisors, on solving for unknowns, and on the importance of primes in determining the number of factors.

Facilitating the Gallery Walk

❖ Form peer review groups to discuss some of their tentative findings from Day Seven.

❖ Confer with students as they finish up work and make posters, asking them to consider the most important things they want to tell their audience.

❖ Conduct a gallery walk to allow students time to reflect and comment on each other's posters.

Facilitating the Math Congress

❖ Convene students at the meeting area to discuss a few important ideas that have surfaced about the importance of primes.

Math Journals

❖ At the end of the congress, provide everyone with some reflective writing time.

Minilesson: A String of Related Problems

Work through each problem one at a time inviting students to share their strategies for each. Use the array model to represent students' thinking. When representing multiplication, the factors are the dimensions and the area inside the array is unknown. When representing division, the dividend is the area and the divisor is the number of rows. The quotient is the number of columns and it is unknown.

The String:

1x17
17/1
13/13
13/1
3 x 3
3x3x3
27/9
3 x ? = 27
How many factors does 27 have?
2x2
2x2x2
4x4
2x2x2x2
8 x ? = 16
How many factors does 16 have?
16/2
2x2x3x3
How many factors does 4 have?
How many factors does 9 have?
How many factors does 36 have?

Behind the Numbers

This string has been carefully constructed to support students to understand how factors and divisors are related, to solve for missing unknowns, and to foster more examination of primes and what happens when they are squared or cubed. At the end students are challenged to examine a case of a prime times a prime. Since 4 has 3 factors and 9 has 3 factors, 36 has 9 factors.

Teacher Note:

Representation is important as you work through this string. You can either use arrays cut from 1 inch square graph paper, or if your students have a good understanding of arrays you can just draw open arrays. The first problem should be represented as 1 row of 17. The area is unknown until students justify that it is also 17. This rectangular array can be used when students solve the next problem. Just erase the dimension across the top that represents the columns, leaving the area of 17 (the dividend) now as known. When students justify that the quotient is 17, write the dimension back in. The next two problems are related similarly but notice that the array is turned. Represent the third problem with 13 rows and only 1 column. When students solve the 4th problem just turn the array 90° so that it now has only 1 row. When you get to 3x3x3, some students are likely to just know it is a cube because of the work they did on Day Seven. If so, just draw a cube and label all three dimensions when they say, "I just know that one. It is a cube and it is 27." 27 is now the volume. Others will likely do 3x3 first, solving the problem as 9x3. Here, draw 9 rows and 3 columns writing 27 as the area (or you can draw 3 of the 3x3 squares next to each other, which effectively also results in a 3x9 array or a 9x3 array depending on where you place the squares.) As you progress with the string, continue to represent what students say. 2x2x2 can be represented as a cube, or as 4x2, or as 2x4. You can also put parentheses around the sections students do first, for example if they solve 2x2x2x2 as 4x4, draw a 4x4 square and represent the equation as (2x2)x(2x2)=4x4. If they solve it as 8x2, draw an 8x2 array and write: (2x2x2)x2= 8x2.

Facilitating the Gallery Walk

Ask students to meet in small review groups (usually comprised of 2 pairs of students), with their journals, and to begin by reading over their journal notes from yesterday. Provide 5 minutes of quiet time for them to do so and then provide discussion time. After about 10 minutes, have students return to work in the original pairs and begin making posters and, as they work, move around and confer. Look for ways to take students' understanding to a deeper level by helping them to justify and generalize their observations and conjectures. As the teacher, you are a mentor. But, you are also a member of the audience. Asking questions will help students clarify their ideas. As mentioned earlier in the unit you can use some of the following questions:

- "What do you want me to understand about what you found out? Can you justify it in a way that convinces me?"
- "How do you think your fellow mathematicians will make sense of your ideas?"
- "What do you know with certainty, and what still puzzles you?"

Remind students that it is not necessary to write about everything they did. The posters are not necessarily explanations of everything that was done (false starts, mistakes, and changes made), but instead are justifications of steps for a complete solution, viable arguments of generalizations, or proofs of conjectures and insights. By providing postering time and a gallery walk, you are providing students with an important opportunity to review and refine their thinking—to read and write a viable mathematical argument. This is one of the standards of mathematical practice and an important purpose of the gallery walk.

Once students have posted their work, remind them that gallery walks should be quiet times so that all mathematicians can read and think before commenting. This time should be taken seriously. Distribute the sticky notes to students and take some yourself, too. During the gallery walk it's important for you to look across the pieces for big ideas and strategies from the landscape, so you can plan which pieces of work to select for the congress.

Facilitating the Math Congress

Review the posters and choose a few that you can use for a discussion that will deepen understanding and support growth along the landscape of learning described in the Overview. But in particular, also look for posters that provide a way to focus conversation on ideas related to the importance of primes, such as:

- All prime numbers have only 2 factors, 1 and itself. 1 is not a prime number because it only has 1 factor.
- Squares of primes have exactly 3 factors. They are the factors of the prime, plus one more, which is the product of the squaring. For example, 3^2 has as its factors 1 and 3, plus 9.
- Cubes of primes have exactly 4 factors. Since squares of primes have 3 factors, when you multiply it again by the same prime number you get one more factor—the new product. It's possible that you may have a few students that start to generalize this idea—that every time you multiply a

prime by itself you get one more factor. [Note: Thus, the number of factors is the exponent plus 1.] While this is not an intended goal for 4th graders, students can surprise us.

- If you multiply one prime number by another prime number, for example 3 x 5, the number of factors in the product is 4. In the case of 3x5 = 15, the product has 4 factors: 1, 3, 5, and 15.

A window into one classroom during the math congress follows:

Inside One Classroom: A Portion of the Math Congress

Camille (the teacher): Anthony and Amirah... You noticed an interesting thing in the squares, didn't you? Come tell us about it.

Anthony: Well, 2x2 is 4, 3x3 is 9, 5x5 is 25, and 7x7 is 49. These all make squares and they all have 3 factors.

Amirah: First we thought all square numbers would do that and we added 36 because that is 6x6, and 100 because that is 10x10. But they didn't work. That's when we realized that 3-factor numbers had to be squares of the primes. See, 11x11 works. It is 121. And the only factors are 1, 121, and 11.

Camille: Turn and talk with your math partner about this for a minute. What do you think about what Anthony and Amirah just said? (*Within a few minutes the room is a buzz of voices.)*

Emilio: They are right. Look! Multiply the prime numbers! Two times 2 makes 4, 3 times 3 makes 9, 5 times 5 makes 25! Those are all square numbers. The three-factor numbers are square numbers of the primes!

Camille: This is so interesting! Why does this happen? Let's look at 9. Why does it only have 3 factors and what are they? Sam?

Sam: The prime only has 2 factors, right? Just 1 and 3. When you do 3x3 to make 9, you get a new number. You get 9. But you can't count 3 twice, so you end up with just 1, 3, and 9. Just 3 factors.

Rafael: And if you double the prime numbers you get a four-factor number. Look at the chart (*pointing to the chart with excitement*). See how the four-factor numbers go? They go 6, 10, then 14. These are four-factor numbers and they are

Author's notes

After a brief discussion on the numbers that students have put in the categories and a check on the factors, Camille turns the congress to a discussion of squares using the work of Anthony and Amirah. She had conferred with them earlier and read their journals last night and she knows they explored squares of primes and this will serve as a nice place to start a discussion on the importance of primes.

Notice how Camille turns the conversation into pair talk at this moment? Doing so provides needed reflection time on some underlying big ideas and will enable more engagement in the conversation as it continues.

Exploring the "why" and justifying that the conjecture generalizes is important. Sam's explanation is a powerful one.

Rafael is thinking of doubling as an addition. Another way to think about doubling is that the original prime number

two times the odd two-factor numbers, 2 times 3, 2 times 5, and 2 times 7. **Sam:** Hey, multiply any two different prime numbers and you get a four-factor number! **Camille:** (elated) Wow! I'm hearing so many neat ideas! So, what do you think the next four-factor number will be? Amirah? **Amirah:** I think 18 because that's 2 times 9." **Sam:** (*looking at the chart he and Emilio have made*) No, it can't be 18. That's a six-factor number. It's 15 I think. And that's 3 times 5. Two primes. **Emilio:** (shaking his head in disagreement) But 15 is an odd number. I don't think odd numbers can be four-factor numbers. **Amirah:** Yes, it is 15! See, 1, 3, 5, and 15. It does have four factors. Both odd and even numbers work. But look, the first number in every column is an even number!	*is being multiplied by 2, which is another prime having only 2 factors.* *Sam generalizes Rafael's idea with multiplication.* *Amirah's answer at first seems to be a logical extension, but as Sam points out, it doesn't work. (9 is not a prime number. It is a square and thus a composite number.)*
Carolina: And I think if you square a three-factor number you get a five-factor number! 4x4 = 16 and it has 5 factors. And 9x9 = 81 and that had 5 factors, too. Just 1, 3, 9, 27..., that's 3x3x3, like we did in the minilesson, ...and 81. **Camille**: Wow, so now we have some good questions to investigate. Let's go back to work and continue investigating.	*Camille knows they need time to explore further, but now they have a multitude of observations and questions that can direct their explorations. She decides it will be more fruitful to send them back to work on some of the ideas further rather than to stay in the congress. A good decision!*

Math Journals

At the end of the congress, provide everyone with some individual reflective writing time. Questions you might ask students to address are:

- Did you hear about an idea in math workshop that you thought was interesting or particularly powerful?
- Is there a new idea that you are now thinking about? How will you start investigating it?

Reflections on the Day

Today your students had the opportunity to deepen their understanding of our number system. The minilesson helped students consider factors as divisors, explore the relationship of multiplication to division, solve for unknowns, and to see the importance of primes in determining the number of factors in a number. The minilesson also helped build a stronger foundation for the work on the investigation they had begun yesterday. As students continued to search for structure and regularity, new questions emerged about the importance of primes. Today you also had another chance to look at your students' work and get a better idea of where each student is travelling on the landscape of learning. Are they factoring flexibly, or are they still challenged by even determining the factors? Do they use the associative property to determine factors? Are they able to use the array as a tool? Remember to track each student's mathematical development on individual landscapes! Tomorrow they will dig even deeper into number theory as they begin exploring triangular numbers!

DAY NINE

TRIANGULAR NUMBERS

Materials Needed

Graph paper

Math Journals

Pencils

Triangular Numbers (Appendix F, one per pair of students)

Markers

Scissors

Today another investigation is introduced. Students learn about the mystery of triangular numbers and the possibility of a hidden double agent. They build a sequence of the triangular numbers and examine patterns in it.

Day Nine Outline

Developing the Context

❖ Tell the story of the mystery of triangular numbers and the possibility of a hidden double agent.

❖ Students build sequences for triangular numbers and examine patterns.

Supporting the Investigation

❖ Note students' strategies as they work and encourage them to make sequences for triangular numbers, to model them on graph paper, and to note what the shape would be if the triangular number were doubled.

Developing the Context

Inform students that there is another mystery for the detectives to crack, this time one that involves INTERPOL. Explain that INTERPOL is an international police organization that fights crime worldwide and it maintains a huge database.

Display Appendix F as you tell the following:

Some numbers have figured out how to transform themselves into triangles! They got into the INTERPOL database and found some interesting information:

Clue #1: A partial sequence for triangular numbers

1, 3, 6, 10, 15, 21,........

Tech Tip:

If you do a search for "Interpol" you will likely find a nice video clip that can be used to develop the context. But, make sure you preview it carefully first to be certain it is appropriate to use with your children. There are clips available as well of kids explaining triangular numbers, but don't use them to develop the context as too much is explained and then there is nothing for students to investigate!

Clue #2: A chart of data

Layer	Total
1	1
2	3
3	6
4	10
5	15
6	
7	
8	
9	
10	

Clue #3: Some drawings showing a possible "double agent"

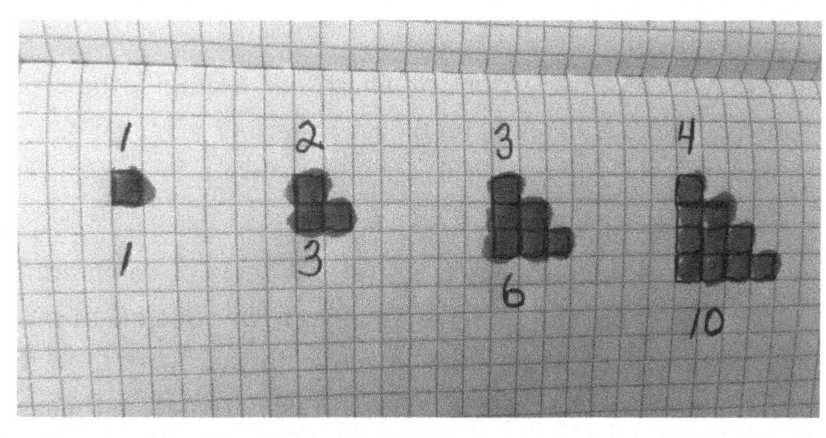

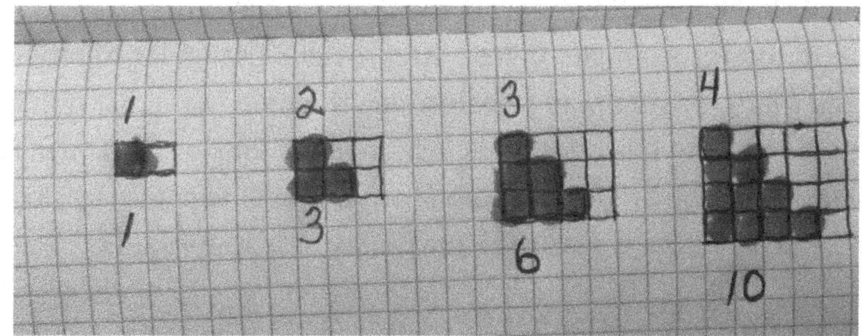

Examine the clues. Look for patterns. How does a triangular number get formed? Is there a double hidden in the rectangle?

Pass out Appendix F, one copy per pair of students. Provide graph paper, markers, pencils, and scissors as tools and send them off in pairs to work on the investigation.

Supporting the Investigation

Provide everyone with time to examine all the clues and try to make sense of them. Don't explain anything about them, just stay in the context reminding students that these were things found in the INTERPOL database. Urge them to work as detectives examining the clues and thinking about how the clues might be related. Then move around and confer. You may note some of the following strategies:

- Most students will likely start by making more pictures using the graph paper. This is a great way to start as they will likely come to realize as they work, that each time a new layer is being added it is one more square than the prior layer. Encourage students to make a connection between the clues. You might ask, "Where is this new layer in the chart, or in the sequence?" In the sequence, the difference is growing accordingly: the difference between 1 and 3 is +2; the difference between 3 and 6 is +3; the difference between 6 and 10 is +4. In the chart, they will likely notice the same thing. The difference between the triangular numbers is growing by one each time. This information will enable students to go beyond needing to draw each consecutive number, and to instead be able to infer what the next number is by adding the new difference, which is 1 more than previous difference.
- Others may note a pattern in the chart. For example, they may note that adding the numbers diagonally produces the new total each time: 1+2 = 3; 3+3=6. See Figure 7.

As you confer with students using this strategy, begin by celebrating what they have noticed. Ask them if they have any ideas why this might be happening. Encourage them to look at the drawings to find the increase in the drawing. Once they understand why their strategy works, note how in their strategy one would have to know the numbers in the prior case in order to know the next. 10 can't be found for example, unless the previous triangular number is known. Challenge them to find a way to determine the next triangular number without needing to know all the prior ones. Ask them to look at the drawings where a rectangle is outlined and wonder aloud what that clue could possibly mean and why there is a comment about the possibility of a double agent.

Layer	Total
1	1
2	3
3	6
4	10
5	15
6	

Figure 7

- Still others may begin with the two drawings and wonder why the second drawing has rectangles outlined. Ask them what the dimensions of the rectangles are and suggest they record that data and see how it compares to the triangular number within it, noting that detectives (and mathematicians) like to record lots of evidence that they notice—sometimes it is helpful later, sometimes not—but recording it down might be very handy later. The rectangles are formed by adding +1 to the second dimension. For example, if one wants to find the 5th triangular number one could multiply 5 by 6 to produce an array of 5x6=30. The triangular number is half of the array. It is 15. The context of the possible "double agent" was designed to help students notice that the triangular number is half of the rectangle.

Facilitating the Math Congress

As students finish exploring and have generated some ideas about triangular numbers, move them into postering. Review the posters as they work and choose a few that you can use for a discussion that will deepen understanding and support growth along the landscape of learning described in the Overview. In particular, look for posters that provide a way to focus conversation on ideas related to the sequence, patterns they have noticed, what numbers they think might come next, and why. Some ideas that would provide for a nice discussion follow:

- Look for a poster where kids describe how each number is growing by adding a new layer that has exactly one more square than the previous layer and who can use this knowledge to predict the next terms in the sequence and draw the next triangular numbers accordingly. By presenting this poster for discussion first, you ensure everyone understands how the numbers are growing and what the next terms will be.
- Follow it with a poster that describes the addition diagonally as shown on the table in Figure 7. Support a discussion on how this strategy is related to the first.
- Lastly, if any students focused on the rectangle and the two triangles within it, have them share what they have noticed. After they share, support a discussion on the dimensions of the rectangle and ask students to consider a way to represent the dimensions. If it feels natural and students are following, you can introduce *n* to represent the dimension on one side of the rectangle and support students to see that the other side is n+1. They should be able to see that cutting the rectangle in half produces the triangle. This produces the general formula for triangular numbers: n (n+1)/2.

Reflection on the Day

Today students were provided with another chance to explore a sequence and to consider how numbers can be thought of as geometric shapes—as triangles, too—not just as squares and cubes. Tomorrow they will have a chance to learn about another sequence—a very special one that can be used to mathematize the propagation of rabbits through generations, and the growth of many animals and objects in nature such as shells, sunflowers, and pinecones. They make spiraling designs of the sequence and then a gallery walk will be held to display and view the art of numbers. A subsequent congress allows students to discuss the insights they had about numbers throughout the unit and as a culmination (or extension) to the unit students have an opportunity to explore several other sequences and to write their own.

DAY TEN

LEONARDO'S NUMBERS

Materials Needed

The Fibonacci Sequence and Spiral (Appendix G, one copy per student)

Number Sequences and Art (Appendix H, one copy per student)

Blockhead: The Life of Fibonacci by Joseph D'Agnese (2010). NY: Henry Holt and Co. and ***Growing Patterns*** by Susan Campbell (2010). Honesdale, PA: Boyds Mills Press (Optional, but nice to use to introduce the context)

Graph paper (poster size)

Drawing Paper

Math Journals

Pencils and Markers

Today begins with the introduction of another sequence of numbers, one that is found all over in nature and has been used by artists through the centuries—the Fibonacci sequence. Students explore the sequence and make art designs and spirals from it. They are also invited to make a display of their own designs using the Fibonacci sequence, invent their own sequences, and describe the mathematics ideas in them.

Day Ten Outline

Developing the Context

- Display a portion of the Fibonacci sequence and invite students to study it and try to determine the rule for it and the next number.
- Read the story *Blockhead: The Life of Fibonacci* and/or *Growing Patterns* to introduce the context. Alternatively, you can just use the story provided in the unit.
- Display Appendix G, showing how the sequence can be used to make a spiral. Show other possible art works and other sequences that students can investigate and invite them to also make sequences of their own and to see if their friends can figure out the rule they have in mind for each.

Supporting the Investigation

- Note students' strategies as they work and support them to produce the designs and sequences they are trying to make.

Gallery Walk and Celebration

- Allow students to find personal ways to display their work and host a parent night where they can share the display.

Developing the Context

To introduce the context, display the following sequence and invite students to examine it for patterns and try to determine what number they think might come next:

1, 1, 2, 3, 5, 8, 13...........

It is 21, because the sequence is formed by adding the last two numbers in the sequence to produce the next: 8+13 = 21. After 21 would come 34 because 13+21 = 34, etc.

Next, read the story about where the sequence came from and why it is so special. *Blockhead: The Life of Fibonacci* by Joseph D'Agnese is a lovely illustrated book that you can use to introduce Fibonacci and the origin of the sequence. *Growing Patterns* by Susan Campbell is a book showing all the places in nature where the numbers are found.

> **Tech Tip:**
>
> If you do a search on YouTube for video on *Fibonacci Numbers in Nature* you will find several clips that can be used to also develop the context. But, make sure you preview clips carefully first to be certain the one you choose is appropriate to use with your children.

Alternatively, you can use the following story:

The sequence is called the Fibonacci sequence. It was developed many, many years ago by a young Italian boy named Leonardo. In Italian, Fibonacci means, "son of Bonaccio." Bonaccio was Leonardo's father's name. Leonardo loved numbers so much that he was always dreaming about them and making up sequences. When he grew up he became a famous mathematician.

The amazing thing about the Fibonacci sequence is that the numbers seem to appear all over in nature. The number of petals in many flowers is usually one of the Fibonacci numbers. The numbers can be used to make beautiful spirals, and these can be found in snails and shells, on the heads of sunflowers, and on the outside of pineapples and pinecones.

Display Appendix G. Using a sheet of chart-size graph paper, demonstrate how to make the spiral using the Fibonacci sequence. Then display Appendix H, showing another possible design using the Fibonacci sequence, as well as other sequences they can explore.

Explain that today is the last day of the unit and that you thought it would be nice to make a big display of all the things they have learned about numbers and to host a Gallery Walk for parents and families. Invite students to make designs, art work, and/or sequences for it, and send them off to work.

> **Tech Tip:**
>
> A fun thing to do is to film short video clips of students talking about a sequence that they were particularly interested in, showing how numbers can be transformed into geometric shapes, or explaining some divisibility rules. You can then play the clips during the Gallery Walk for families to see.

Supporting the Investigation

Provide everyone with time to explore and design. Students can make spirals, write new sequences and invite friends to figure them out, or revisit their posters from prior days and revise or add to them. As you move around help students think about what they would like to make and display for families to see. Then confer and support them as they work.

Reflection on the Unit

"...the feeling of mathematical beauty, of the harmony of numbers and of forms, of geometric elegance. It is a genuinely aesthetic feeling, which all mathematicians know."

Henri Poincare

As your students progressed through the unit, you took them on a journey filled with wonder and mystery. They investigated common multiples and factors, constructed divisibility rules, explored squares, cubes, and composites, and uncovered the beauty of primes. They transformed quantities and sequences into elegant geometric forms, establishing a unity to what had seemed previously to be separate strands of mathematics. Numbers will never be the same to them again; they will be used to mathematize the world around them and to characterize the beautiful patterns in nature.

In this unit, students have been provided with many opportunities to examine patterns, functions, and structures in our number system. They collected evidence of regularities and were faced with the cracking of mathematical mysteries and the establishing of proofs for their solutions. In doing so, they experienced the feeling of mathematical beauty and saw the harmony of numbers and forms. And, as young mathematicians at work, they were awed by the genuinely aesthetic feeling so poignantly expressed by the mathematician, Henri Poincare, in the epigraph.

Appendix A

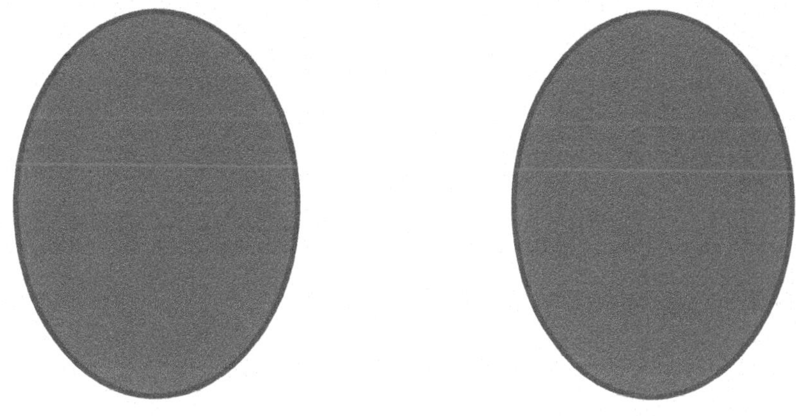

Detectives________________&________________

Appendix B (1 of 3)

Mystery #1: The Case of #322

A crime was committed at #322 and footprints were found at the point, just under a wharf along a deserted beach. Footprints have also been found at certain points along the way pointing to other stopping places. In fact, evidence shows where the possible stopping points are for each of three suspects. The three suspects are #2, #3, and #4. Who could have stopped at #322?

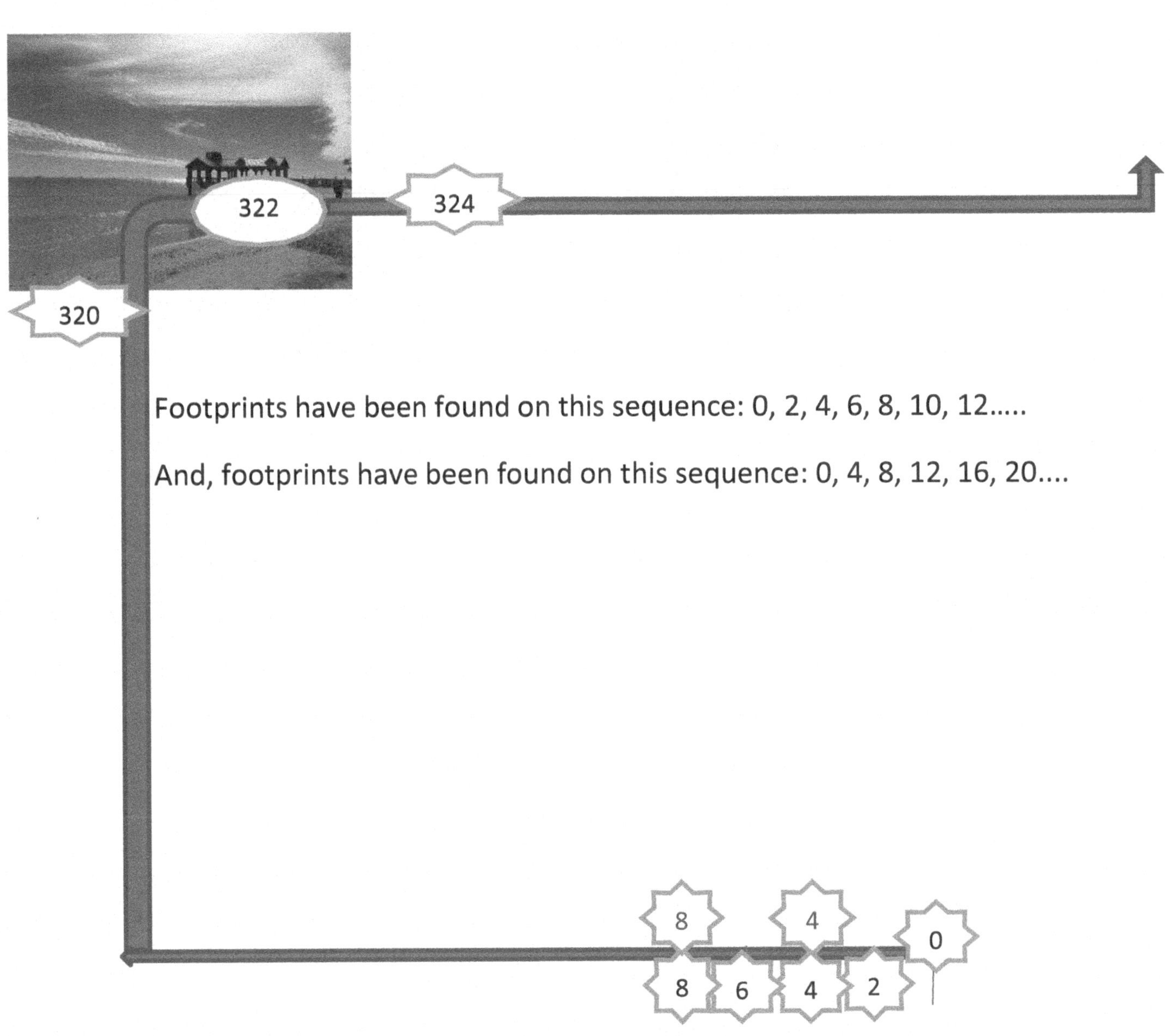

Appendix B (2 of 3)

Check out the computer database for more clues.

x2

In	Out
1	2
2	4
3	6
4	8
5	
6	
10	
11	
50	
	200
	300
	322

x3

In	Out
1	3
2	6
3	9
4	12
5	15
6	18
9	
10	
	99
	120
	240
100	

Build a computer database for x4

Appendix B (3 of 3)

Is there a way to tell ahead if a number is divisible by 2?

What about 4?

Appendix C (1 of 2)

Agent #9 has organized a Secret Agent's meeting in his favorite meeting place:

location  , in the woods inside the trunk of an old giant redwood tree.

The purpose of the meeting is for the agents to share their secret codes, write them down, and bury them together at the location. All agents must use their codes to get in. Agent #9 likes this spot because he knows he can get there easily. He sees his secret code right away: the sum of the digits in location 90 is 9+0 =9. All he needs to do is take 10 steps along the path and he is there! He writes his code down and explains why summing the digits works. He is ready for the meeting.

1	9
2	18
3	27
4	36
5	45
6	54
7	63
8	72
9	81
10	90

Appendix C (2 of 2)

Agents #2, #3, #4, #5, #6, and #10 all get the message about the meeting. They wonder, "Will they all be able to get in? Will their secret codes get them there?"

Draw the pathways for these agents and see where their steps take them. Or, make some databases to help. Once you know the code, write it down and be ready to present evidence of your solution for each.

X2

In	Out

x3

In	Out

x4

In	Out

x5

In	Out

x6

In	Out

x10

In	Out

Appendix D

The Transformers

The secret agents have learned that their codes have been cracked!

So, to disguise themselves, they have started to use their powers to transform themselves into shapes. For example, when 2 arrives on location #4 and meets 4, she transforms herself into a square, and when she arrives on 8, she transforms herself into a cube.

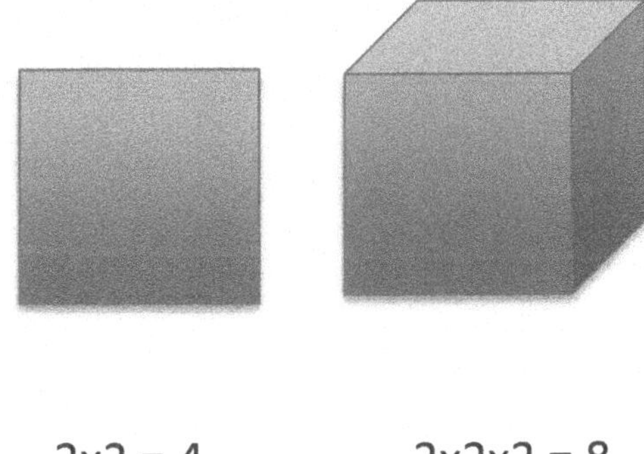

2x2 = 4 2x2x2 = 8

The agents all start making two sequences: one for square numbers; one for cube numbers.

This is what they have so far:

1, 4, 9, 16, 25.....

1, 8, 27, 64, 125....

Which sequence is which? And, what comes next in these sequences?

Are there any spots (numbers) that can be both a square and a cube?

Appendix E

1-Factor Numbers	2-Factor Numbers	3-Factor Numbers	4-Factor Numbers	5-Factor Numbers	6-Factor Numbers	7-Factor Numbers	8-Factor Numbers	9-Factor Numbers	10-Factor Numbers

Appendix F

Some numbers have figured out how to transform themselves into triangles! They got into the INTERPOL database and found some interesting information:

Clue #1: A partial sequence for triangular numbers

1, 3, 6, 10, 15, 21,……..

Clue #2: A chart of data

Layer	Total
1	1
2	3
3	6
4	10
5	15
6	
7	
8	
9	
10	

Clue #3: Some drawings showing a possible "double agent"

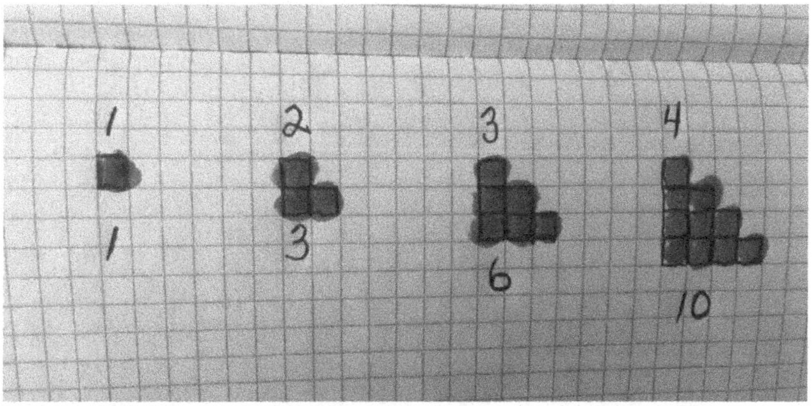

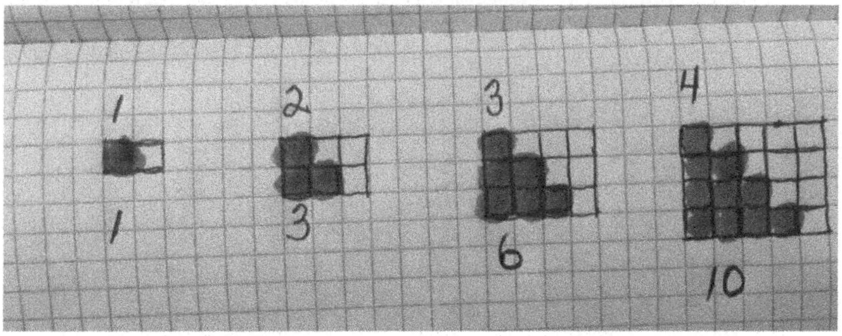

Is there a double hidden in the rectangle?

Examine the clues. Look for patterns. How does a triangular number get formed?

Appendix G

The Fibonacci Sequence

1, 1, 2, 3, 5, 8, 13……… What comes next?

Transforming into a spiral!

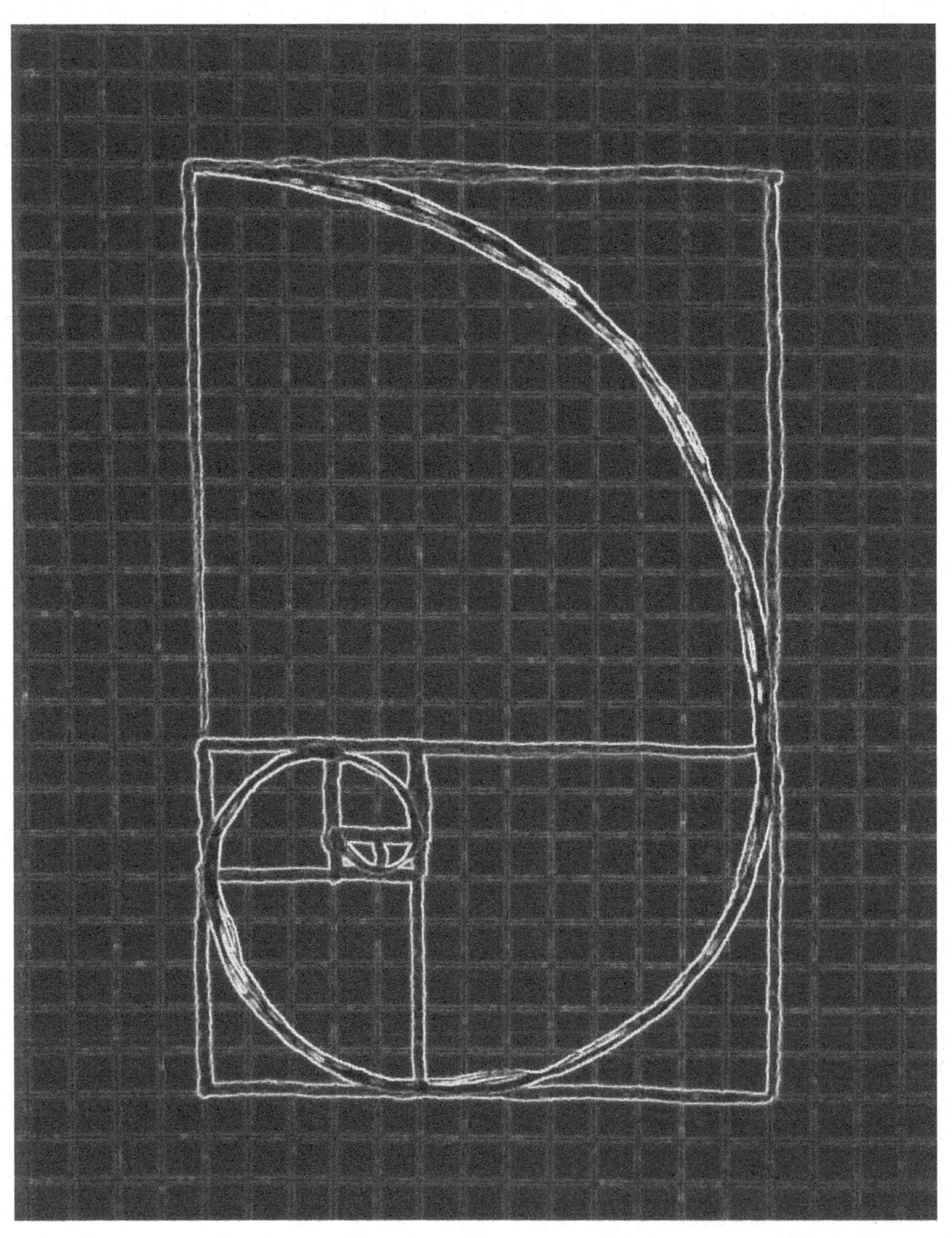

Appendix H (1 of 2)

More Art Using the Fibonacci Sequence

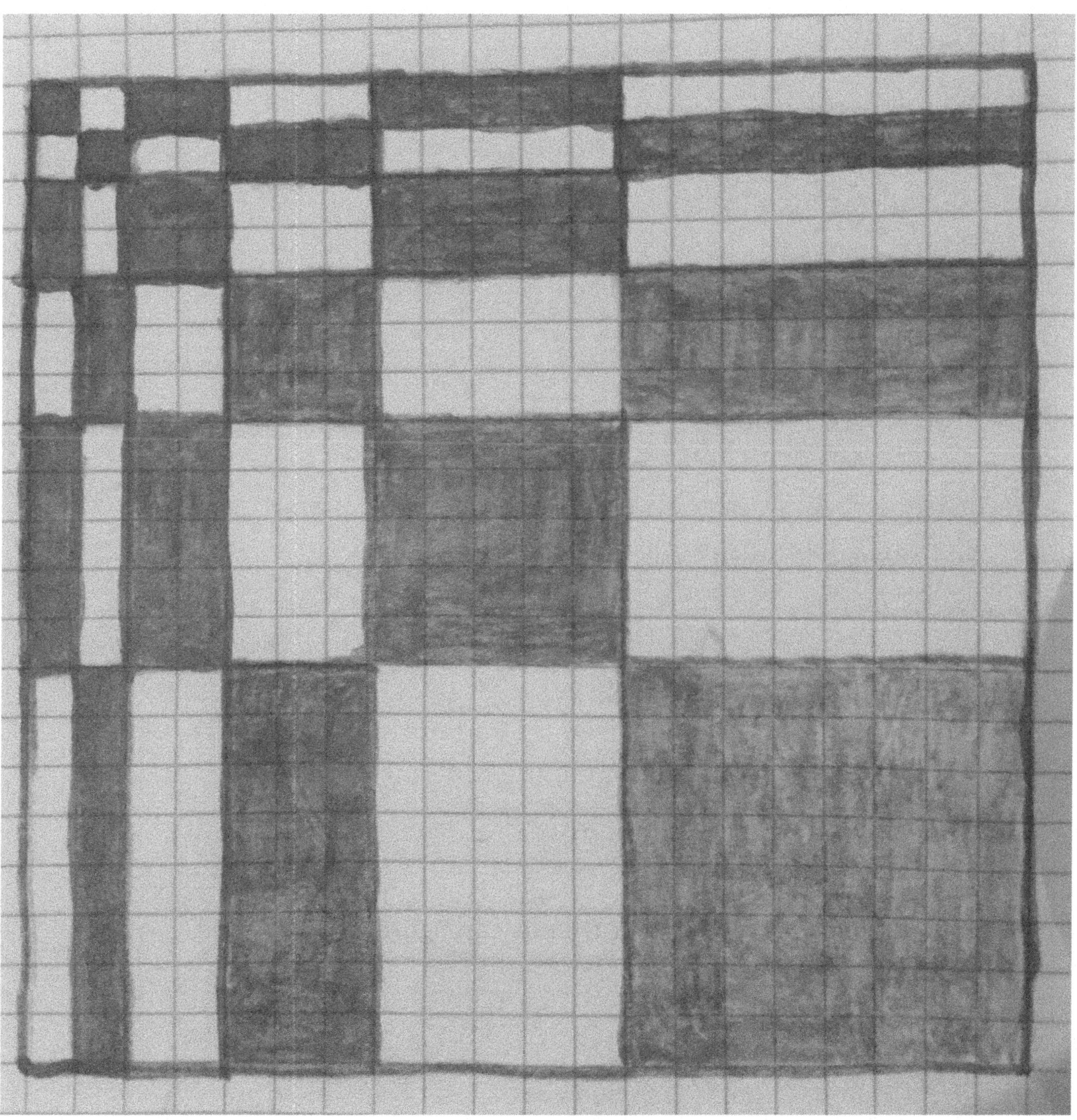

Appendix H (2 of 2)

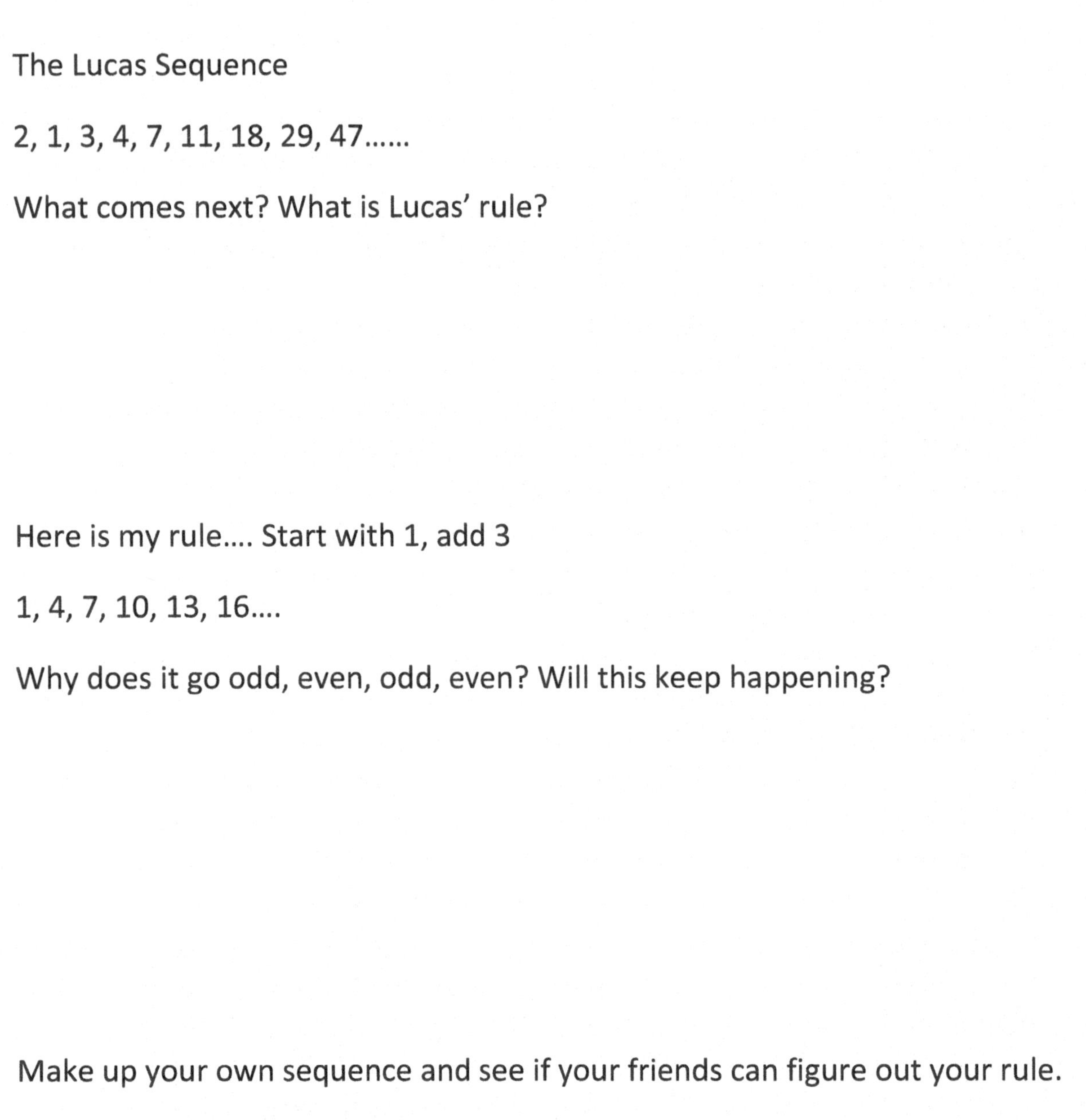

The Lucas Sequence

2, 1, 3, 4, 7, 11, 18, 29, 47......

What comes next? What is Lucas' rule?

Here is my rule.... Start with 1, add 3

1, 4, 7, 10, 13, 16....

Why does it go odd, even, odd, even? Will this keep happening?

Make up your own sequence and see if your friends can figure out your rule.

Made in USA - Kendallville, IN
32820_9781733532105